Career Ideas for Kids Who Like Talking

DIANE LINDSEY REEVES
WITH
NANCY HEUBECK

Illustrations by
NANCY BOND

CAREER IDEAS FOR KIDS WHO LIKE TALKING

Checkmark Books
An imprint of Facts On File, Inc.
11 Penn Plaza
New York NY 10001

Library of Congress Cataloging-in-Publication Data

Reeves, Diane Lindsey, 1959–
Talking / Diane Lindsey Reeves; with Nancy Heubeck.
p. cm.—(Career ideas for kids who like)
Includes bibliographical references and index.
Summary: In addition to information on such diverse occupations as air traffic controller, minister, and speech pathologist, contains exercises and activities to rate aptitudes and interests.
ISBN 0-8160-3683-7 (hardcover).—ISBN 0-8160-3689-6 (pbk.)
1. Vocational guidance—Juvenile literature. 2. Occupations—Juvenile literature. 3. Professions—Juvenile literature. [1. Vocational guidance. 2. Occupations.] I. Heubeck, Nancy. II. Title. III. Series: Reeves, Diane Lindsey, 1959– Career ideas for kids who like.
HF5381.2.R43.R38 1998
331.7'02—dc21 97-50075

Checkmark Books are available at special discounts when purchased in bulk quantities for businesses, associations, institutions, or sales promotions. Please call our Special Sales Department in New York at 212/967-8800 or 800/322-8755.

You can find Facts On File on the World Wide Web at http://www.factsonfile.com

Text and cover design by Smart Graphics
Illustrations by Nancy Bond

This book is printed on acid-free paper.

Printed in the United States of America

MP FOF 10 9 8 7 6 5 4 3 2

(pbk) 10 9 8 7 6 5 4 3 2

This book is dedicated to
my sisters,
Denise Leafgren
and
Gayle Bryan
Two of my favorite people to talk to!
—DLR

To patient teachers everywhere who believe in
the promise, abilities, and hopes of each student,
and to my son Daniel, my inspiration.
May you always fulfill the promises
you make to yourself.
—NH

A million thanks to the people who took the time to share their career stories and provide photos for this book:

Sue Beeson
Bob Davis
Robert Gelinas
Debby Harris
Jerome Jewell
John Kehl
Libby Adler Mages
Mark Miller
Scott Moore
Julie Mordecai
Gregory Mueller
Gail S. Schoettler
Carrie Sherr
Tim Stiers
Laura Woloch

Also, special thanks to the design team of Smart Graphics, Nancy Bond, and Cathy Rincon for bringing the Career Ideas for Kids series to life with their creative talent.

Finally, much appreciation and admiration is due to my editor, Nicole Bowen, whose vision and attention to detail increased the quality of this project in many wonderful ways.

CONTENTS

You're young. Most of your life is still ahead of you. How are you supposed to know what you want to be when you grow up?

You're right: 10, 11, 12, 13, is a bit young to know exactly what and where and how you're going to do whatever it is you're going to do as an adult. But, it's the perfect time to start making some important discoveries about who you are, what you like to do, and what you do best. It's the ideal time to start thinking about what you *want* to do.

Make a choice! If you get a head start now, you may avoid setbacks and mistakes later on.

When it comes to picking a career, you've basically got two choices.

CHOICE A

Wait until you're in college to start figuring out what you want to do. Even then you still may not decide what's up your alley, so you graduate and jump from job to job still searching for something you really like.

Hey, it could work. It might be fun. Lots of (probably most) people do it this way.

The problem is that if you pick Choice A, you may end up settling for second best. You may miss out on a meaningful education, satisfying work, and the rewards of a focused and well-planned career.

You have another choice to consider.

CHOICE B

Start now figuring out your options and thinking about the things that are most important in your life's work: Serving others? Staying true to your values? Making lots of money? Enjoying your work? Your young years are the perfect time to mess around with different career ideas without messing up your life.

Reading this book is a great idea for kids who choose B. It's a first step toward choosing a career that matches your skills, interests, and lifetime goals. It will help you make a plan for tailoring your junior and high school years to fit your career dreams. To borrow a jingle from the U.S. Army—using this book is a way to discover how to "be all that you can be."

Ready for the challenge of Choice B? If so, read the next section to find out how this book can help start you on your way.

HOW TO USE THIS BOOK

This isn't a book about interesting careers that other people have. It's a book about interesting careers that you can have.

Of course, it won't do you a bit of good to just read this book. To get the whole shebang, you're going to have to jump in with both feet, roll up your sleeves, put on your thinking cap—whatever it takes—to help you do these three things:

- **Discover** what you do best and enjoy the most. (This is the secret ingredient for finding work that's perfect for you.)

- **Explore** ways to match your interests and abilities with career ideas.
- **Experiment** with lots of different ideas until you find the ideal career. (It's like trying on all kinds of hats to see which ones fit!)

Use this book as a road map to some exciting career destinations. Here's what to expect in the chapters that follow.

GET IN GEAR!

First stop: self-discovery. These activities will help you uncover important clues about the special traits and abilities that make you *you*. When you are finished you will have developed a personal Skill Set that will help guide you to career ideas in the next chapter.

TAKE A TRIP!

Next stop: exploration. Cruise down the career idea highway and find out about a variety of career ideas that are especially appropriate for people who like talking. Use the Skill Set chart at the beginning of each entry to match your own interests with those required for success on the job.

MAKE A VERBAL DETOUR!

Here's your chance to explore up-and-coming opportunities in communications and electronics as well as the tried-and-true fields of writing and teaching.

Just when you thought you'd seen it all, here come dozens of interesting talking ideas to add to the career mix. Charge up your career search by learning all you can about some of these opportunities.

DON'T STOP NOW!

Third stop: experimentation. The library, the telephone, a computer, and a mentor—four keys to a successful career planning adventure. Use them well, and before long you'll be on the trail of some hot career ideas.

WHAT'S NEXT?

Make a plan! Chart your course (or at least the next stop) with these career planning road maps. Whether you're moving full steam ahead with a great idea or get slowed down at a yellow light of indecision, these road maps will keep you moving forward toward a great future.

Use a pencil—you're bound to make a detour or two along the way. But, hey, you've got to start somewhere.

HOORAY! YOU DID IT!

Some final rules of the road before sending you off to new adventures.

SOME FUTURE DESTINATIONS

This section lists a few career planning tools you'll want to know about.

You've got a lot of ground to cover in this phase of your career planning journey. Start your engines and get ready for an exciting adventure!

Career planning is a lifelong journey. There's usually more than one way to get where you're going, and there are often some interesting detours along the way. But, you have to start somewhere. So, rev up and find out all you can about you—one-of-a-kind, specially designed you. That's the first stop on what can be the most exciting trip of your life!

To get started, complete the two exercises described below.

WATCH FOR SIGNS ALONG THE WAY

Road signs help drivers figure out how to get where they want to go. They provide clues about direction, road conditions, and safety. Your career road signs will provide clues about who you are, what you like, and what you do best. These clues can help you decide where to look for the career ideas that are best for you.

Complete the following statements to make them true for you. There are no right or wrong answers. Jot down the response that describes you best. Your answers will provide important clues about career paths you should explore.

Please Note: If this book does not belong to you, write your responses on a separate sheet of paper.

On my last report card, I got the best grade in __________.

On my last report card, I got the worst grade in __________.

I am happiest when ______________________________.

Something I can do for hours without getting bored is ______________________________.

Something that bores me out of my mind is ______________________________.

My favorite class is ______________________.

My least favorite class is ____________________.

The one thing I'd like to accomplish with my life is ______________________________.

My favorite thing to do after school is ______.

My least favorite thing to do after school is ______________________________.

Something I'm really good at is ______________.

Something that is really tough for me to do is ______________________________.

My favorite adult person is ________________ because ______________________________.

When I grow up ______________________________.

The kinds of books I like to read are about ______________________________.

The kinds of videos I like to watch are about ______________________________.

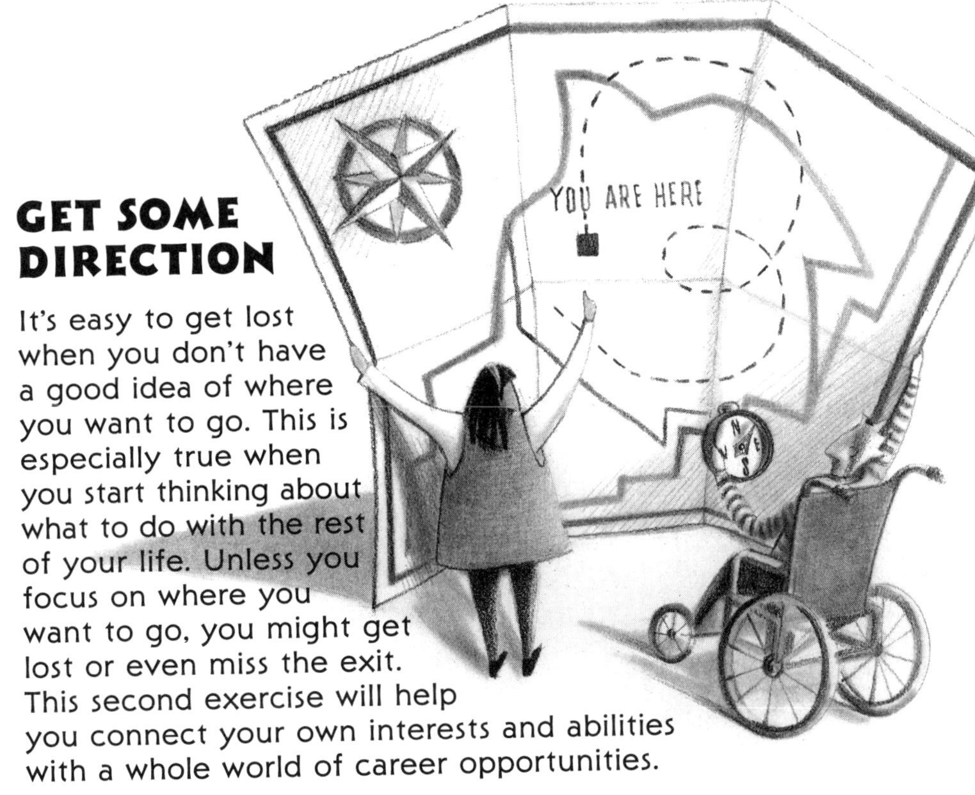

GET SOME DIRECTION

It's easy to get lost when you don't have a good idea of where you want to go. This is especially true when you start thinking about what to do with the rest of your life. Unless you focus on where you want to go, you might get lost or even miss the exit. This second exercise will help you connect your own interests and abilities with a whole world of career opportunities.

Mark the activities that you enjoy doing or would enjoy doing if you had the chance. Be picky. Don't mark ideas that you wish you would do, mark only those that you would really do. For instance, if the idea of skydiving sounds appealing, but you'd never do it because you are terrified of heights, don't mark it.

Please Note: If this book does not belong to you, write your responses on a separate sheet of paper.

- ❑ 1. Rescue a cat stuck in a tree
- ❑ 2. Paint a mural on the cafeteria wall
- ❑ 3. Run for student council
- ❑ 4. Send e-mail to a "pen pal" in another state
- ❑ 5. Find out all there is to know about the American Revolution
- ❑ 6. Survey your classmates to find out what they do after school
- ❑ 7. Try out for the school play
- ❑ 8. Dissect a frog and identify the different organs
- ❑ 9. Play baseball, soccer, football, or _________ (fill in your favorite sport)

- ❑ 10. Talk on the phone to just about anyone who will talk back
- ❑ 11. Try foods from all over the world—Thailand, Poland, Japan, etc.
- ❑ 12. Write poems about things that are happening in your life
- ❑ 13. Create a really scary haunted house to take your friends through on Halloween
- ❑ 14. Bake a cake and decorate it for your best friend's birthday
- ❑ 15. Sell enough advertisements for the school yearbook to win a trip to Walt Disney World
- ❑ 16. Simulate an imaginary flight through space on your computer screen
- ❑ 17. Collect stamps, coins, baseball cards, or whatever and organize them into a fancy display
- ❑ 18. Build model airplanes, boats, doll houses, or anything from kits
- ❑ 19. Teach your friends a new dance routine
- ❑ 20. Watch the stars come out at night and see how many constellations you can find
- ❑ 21. Watch baseball, soccer, football, or _____ (fill in your favorite sport) on TV
- ❑ 22. Give a speech in front of the entire school
- ❑ 23. Plan the class field trip to Washington, D.C.
- ❑ 24. Read everything in sight, including the back of the cereal box
- ❑ 25. Figure out "who dunnit" in a mystery story
- ❑ 26. Make a poster announcing the school football game
- ❑ 27. Think up a new way to make the lunch line move faster and explain it to the cafeteria staff
- ❑ 28. Put together a multimedia show for a school assembly using music and lots of pictures and graphics
- ❑ 29. Visit historic landmarks like the Statue of Liberty and Civil War battlegrounds
- ❑ 30. Invest your allowance in the stock market and keep track of how it does
- ❑ 31. Go to the ballet or opera every time you get the chance

- ❑ 32. Do experiments with a chemistry set
- ❑ 33. Keep score at your sister's Little League game
- ❑ 34. Use lots of funny voices when reading stories to children
- ❑ 35. Ride on airplanes, trains, boats—anything that moves
- ❑ 36. Interview the new exchange student for an article in the school newspaper
- ❑ 37. Build your own treehouse
- ❑ 38. Visit an art museum and pick out your favorite painting
- ❑ 39. Play Monopoly® in an all-night championship challenge
- ❑ 40. Make a chart on the computer to show how much soda students buy from the school vending machines each week
- ❑ 41. Find out all you can about your family ancestors and make a family tree
- ❑ 42. Keep track of how much your team earns to buy new uniforms
- ❑ 43. Play an instrument in the school band or orchestra
- ❑ 44. Put together a 1,000-piece puzzle
- ❑ 45. Write stories about sports for the school newspaper
- ❑ 46. Listen to other people talk about their problems
- ❑ 47. Imagine yourself in exotic places

- ❑ 48. Hang around bookstores and libraries
- ❑ 49. Play harmless practical jokes on April Fools' Day
- ❑ 50. Take photographs at the school talent show
- ❑ 51. Make money by setting up your own business—paper route, lemonade stand, etc.
- ❑ 52. Create an imaginary city using a computer
- ❑ 53. Look for Native American artifacts and arrowheads
- ❑ 54. Do 3-D puzzles
- ❑ 55. Keep track of the top 10 songs of the week
- ❑ 56. Train your dog to do tricks
- ❑ 57. Make play-by-play announcements at the school football game
- ❑ 58. Answer the phones during a telethon to raise money for orphans
- ❑ 59. Be an exchange student in another country
- ❑ 60. Write down all your secret thoughts and favorite sayings in a journal
- ❑ 61. Jump out of an airplane (with a parachute, of course)
- ❑ 62. Use a video camera to make your own movies
- ❑ 63. Get your friends together to help clean up your town after a hurricane
- ❑ 64. Spend your summer at a computer camp learning lots of new computer programs

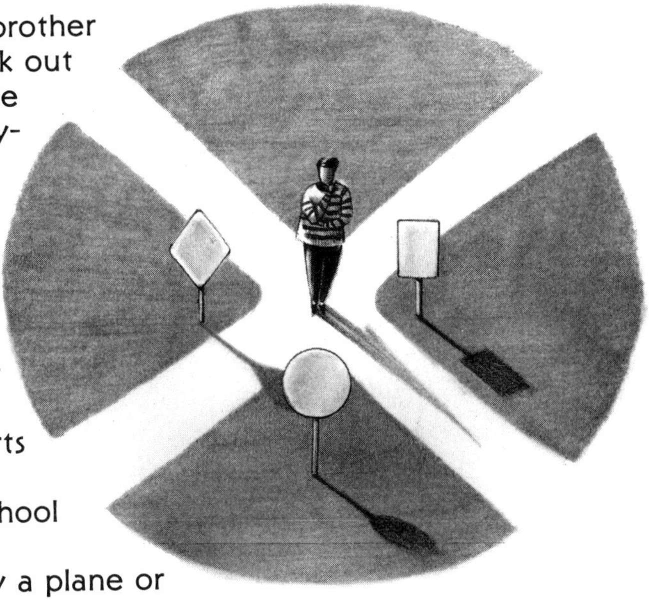

- ❑ 65. Help your little brother or sister make ink out of blueberry juice
- ❑ 66. Build bridges, skyscrapers, and other structures out of LEGO®s
- ❑ 67. Plan a concert in the park for little kids
- ❑ 68. Collect different kinds of rocks
- ❑ 69. Help plan a sports tournament
- ❑ 70. Be DJ for the school dance
- ❑ 71. Learn how to fly a plane or sail a boat
- ❑ 72. Write funny captions for pictures in the school yearbook
- ❑ 73. Scuba dive to search for buried treasure
- ❑ 74. Sketch pictures of your friends
- ❑ 75. Pick out neat stuff to sell at the school store
- ❑ 76. Answer your classmates' questions about how to use the computer
- ❑ 77. Make a timeline showing important things that happened during the year
- ❑ 78. Draw a map showing how to get to your house from school
- ❑ 79. Make up new words to your favorite songs
- ❑ 80. Take a hike and name the different kinds of trees, birds, or flowers
- ❑ 81. Referee intramural basketball games
- ❑ 82. Join the school debate team
- ❑ 83. Make a poster with postcards from all the places you went on your summer vacation
- ❑ 84. Write down stories that your grandparents tell you about when they were young

CALCULATE THE CLUES

Now is your chance to add it all up. Each of the 12 boxes on these pages contains an interest area that is common to both your world and the world of work. Follow these directions to discover your personal Skill Set:

1. Find all of the numbers that you checked on pages 9–13 in the boxes below and X them. Work your way all the way through number 84.
2. Go back and count the Xs marked for each interest area. Write that number in the space that says "total."
3. Find the interest area with the highest total and put a number one in the "Rank" blank of that box. Repeat this process for the next two highest scoring areas. Rank the second highest as number two and the third highest as number three.
4. If you have more than three strong areas, choose the three that are most important and interesting to you.

Remember: If this book does not belong to you, write your responses on a separate sheet of paper.

ADVENTURE

❑ 1
❑ 13
❑ 25
❑ 37
❑ 49
❑ 61
❑ 73

Total: _____
Rank: _____

ART

❑ 2
❑ 14
❑ 26
❑ 38
❑ 50
❑ 62
❑ 74

Total: _____
Rank: _____

BUSINESS

❑ 3
❑ 15
❑ 27
❑ 39
❑ 51
❑ 63
❑ 75

Total: _____
Rank: _____

COMPUTERS

- ❑ 4
- ❑ 16
- ❑ 28
- ❑ 40
- ❑ 52
- ❑ 64
- ❑ 76

Total: _____
Rank: _____

HISTORY

- ❑ 5
- ❑ 17
- ❑ 29
- ❑ 41
- ❑ 53
- ❑ 65
- ❑ 77

Total: _____
Rank: _____

MATH

- ❑ 6
- ❑ 18
- ❑ 30
- ❑ 42
- ❑ 54
- ❑ 66
- ❑ 78

Total: _____
Rank: _____

MUSIC/DANCE

- ❑ 7
- ❑ 19
- ❑ 31
- ❑ 43
- ❑ 55
- ❑ 67
- ❑ 79

Total: _____
Rank: _____

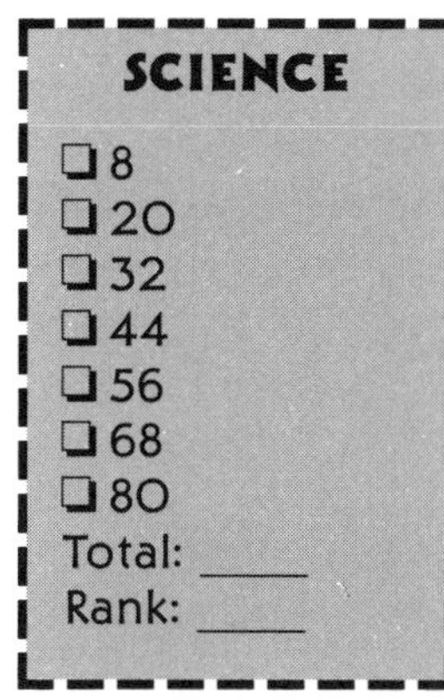

SCIENCE

- ❑ 8
- ❑ 20
- ❑ 32
- ❑ 44
- ❑ 56
- ❑ 68
- ❑ 80

Total: _____
Rank: _____

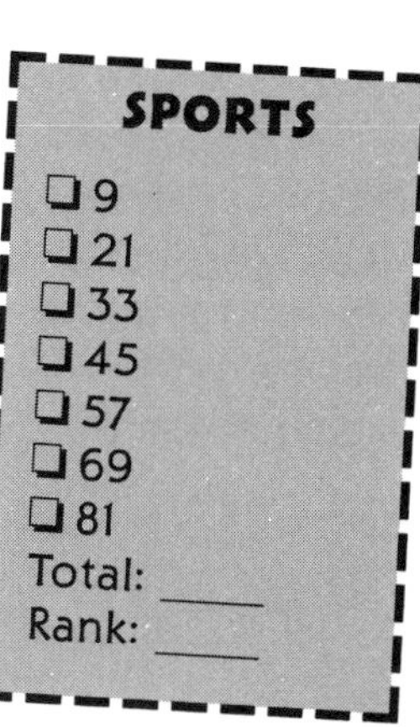

SPORTS

- ❑ 9
- ❑ 21
- ❑ 33
- ❑ 45
- ❑ 57
- ❑ 69
- ❑ 81

Total: _____
Rank: _____

TALKING

- ❑ 10
- ❑ 22
- ❑ 34
- ❑ 46
- ❑ 58
- ❑ 70
- ❑ 82

Total: _____
Rank: _____

TRAVEL

- ❑ 11
- ❑ 23
- ❑ 35
- ❑ 47
- ❑ 59
- ❑ 71
- ❑ 83

Total: _____
Rank: _____

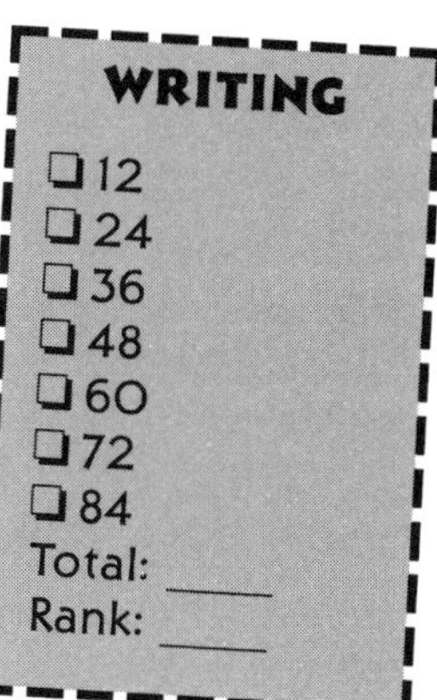

WRITING

- ❑ 12
- ❑ 24
- ❑ 36
- ❑ 48
- ❑ 60
- ❑ 72
- ❑ 84

Total: _____
Rank: _____

What are your top three interest areas? List them here (or on a separate piece of paper).

1. ____________________

2. ____________________

3. ____________________

This is your personal Skill Set and provides important clues about the kinds of work you're most likely to enjoy. Remember it and look for career ideas with a skill set that matches yours most closely.

Cruise down the career idea highway and enjoy in-depth profiles of some of the interesting options in this field. Keep in mind all that you've discovered about yourself so far. Find the careers that match your own Skill Set first. Then keep considering the other ideas—exploration is the name of this game.

Talking careers are based on exceptionally good communication skills. Keep in mind that communication skills are a two-way street with talking going one way and listening coming back. Good communicators can't have one skill without the other. They're a natural pair—sort of like shoes and socks.

As you browse through the following talking career ideas, you may be surprised to discover that many communication careers share two common denominators. First, communicators of all kinds use computers. Talkers—whether on the phone, the radio, the television, or in person—rely heavily on information and need a way to keep track of it.

The second common denominator is that talkers like people. Their jobs often require that they spend lots of time with people, so it really helps if they actually like the people they are working with.

Talking careers open up a wide variety of options. Some careers require college; some don't. Some careers can be done with just a little bit of training on the job; others require extensive training. Most of all, these careers require you to have fun while you talk.

As you read about the following careers, imagine yourself doing each job and ask yourself the following questions:

- Would I like it?
- Would I be good at it?
- Is it the stuff my career dreams are made of?

If so, make a quick exit to explore what it involves, try it out, check it out, and get acquainted.

Buckle up and enjoy the trip!

Air Traffic Controller

SKILL SET

- ✔ ADVENTURE
- ✔ MATH
- ✔ TALKING

SHORTCUTS

GO visit your local airport and get acquainted with the various types of aircraft that fly in and out on a regular basis.

READ *Things That Go Bump in the Flight* by Captain Robert Welch (Cincinnati, Ohio: Betterway Publications, 1987).

TRY putting together model airplanes and learning to distinguish the special features of each type of aircraft.

WHAT IS AN AIR TRAFFIC CONTROLLER?

Picture a police officer directing traffic. Hold that thought and replace the well-marked streets with huge runways and the big, blue, wide-open sky. That, in a nutshell, is what air traffic controllers do. They are responsible for keeping planes a safe distance from each other, both in the air and on the ground at the airport. They help pilots keep on course during flight and route them in the safest way possible. Assuring happy and safe takeoffs and landings is their number-one concern.

Another way to visualize this demanding profession is to think of a juggler keeping several balls in the air at once. It's the same concept for an air traffic controller, except that instead of harmless rubber balls, they are juggling several airplanes full of people and other precious cargo. Efficiency, organization, competency, and total concentration are key attributes that contribute to getting planes and people where they need to be—on time.

Additionally, air traffic controllers must stay in top physical and mental shape to withstand the stresses and demands of the job. They must possess good communication skills and must be able to speak in clear, distinct voices. With so many planes coming and going, the ability to think fast, coupled with exceptional decision-making skills, is an absolute must.

There are three types of controllers. One controller, the enroute controller, keeps in touch with planes while they are between airports. These controllers work in one of 24 special centers across the country in locations away from airports. They make sure planes stay in their "lanes" while they are flying at altitudes at or above 17,000 feet. The typical center is responsible for more than 100,000 square miles of airspace.

Another controller, called the terminal controller, directs traffic while planes approach, take off, and land at his or her airport. They generally control air traffic flying below 17,000 feet within about 20 miles of the airport. They work in the control towers and radar control rooms.

The tower controller, the third type of controller, makes sure that pilots flying within 5 to 10 miles of the airport have all the information they need for a safe flight: The tower controller provides information about weather and current airport conditions that might affect takeoffs and landings. These controllers must often provide advice based on their own observations and experience.

All controllers use radar and other high-tech equipment to do their jobs. Computers play a big part in helping controllers keep planes on course and on schedule. All controllers also work under fairly stressful conditions in a high-energy environment. And one other common ingredient is shared by all types of controllers: There is no room for mistakes!

To become an air traffic controller you must take lots of tests both before you get the job and after. College is not a must, but you will need to have some work experience. Aptitude exams must be passed. There are some age limitations as well. Top physical condition and mental readiness are key requirements. Candidates must be free of anything that could keep them from performing at their best day after day; no drugs or alcohol are allowed here!

Trainees go through the Federal Aviation Administration's Academy in Oklahoma. There they learn about the regulations, the equipment, and how planes fly. They also gain experience in a simulated control tower environment. Once the training is completed, trainees must pass another test before officially qualifying as air traffic controllers.

It isn't an easy job, but air traffic controllers are a vital link in keeping the skies safe and bringing the world closer together.

TRY IT OUT

AIRPORT IN A BOX

Construct a model of the nearest airport. Cut the sides of a large box down to a height of about 6 inches and use poster board and markers to define the space. Use graph paper to sketch out the elements. Some important considerations include, How large is the airport? How many runways does it have? Do those runways go north and south or east and west? Why do they face the way they do?

READ ALL ABOUT IT

For a better understanding of how planes fly, why they fly, and how they navigate, read some of the following books.

Eichenberger, Jerry A. *Cross-Country Flying.* New York: McGraw-Hill, 1995.

Lee, Lincoln. *Three Dimensional Darkness.* Boston: Little, Brown and Company, 1962.

Nahum, Andrew. *Flying Machine: An Eyewitness Book.* New York: Alfred A. Knopf, 1990.

The Visual Dictionary of Flight. New York: DK Publishing, Inc., 1992.

"CONTROL TOWER THIS IS . . ."

Here's your chance to try your skill in a simulated air traffic situation, compliments of the government. Get on-line at http://olias.arc.nasa.gov/cognition/research/freeflgt.html. Once there, you'll have the chance to observe a free-flight air traffic display and predict which two planes are destined to conflict. You'll also get the chance to reroute the planes without creating new conflicts.

ON-LINE DESTINATIONS

Aspiring air traffic controllers can eavesdrop on some important professional shoptalk at http://www.avsim.com. The Squawkbox Forum is where practicing air traffic controllers voice concerns and talk about issues related to their work.

The Federal Aviation Agency (FAA) is the "boss" in charge of all aspects of air safety. They make the rules that air traffic controllers follow. The FAA also has an informative website; stop by for a visit at http://www.faa.gov.

WANTED: FAA TRAFFIC CONTROLLERS

Once you've reached the decision to become an air traffic controller, you may want to invest a few dollars in an information kit that should answer many of your questions about this profession. The kit includes advice on how to become an FAA air traffic controller; instructions on how, when, and where to apply; and a sample application packet. To order an air traffic controller career package, write to PJP Information Guides, P.O. Box 400-IA, Commack, New York 11725-0400.

For those who prefer the low- and no-cost route, you can request from any U.S. Office of Personnel Management Job Information Center a pamphlet that provides general information about controllers and instructions for submitting an application. For the number of the office nearest you, call 800-555-1212.

CHECK IT OUT

National Air Traffic Controllers Association
1150 17th Street NW, Suite 701
Washington, D.C. 20036

Superintendent of Documents
U.S. Government Printing Office
Retail Distribution Division
8610 Cherry Lane
Laurel, Maryland 20707
Request the FAA Aviation Education and Space Materials brochure.

GET ACQUAINTED

Gregory Mueller, Air Traffic Controller

CAREER PATH

CHILDHOOD ASPIRATION: To become a comedian.

FIRST JOB: Worked as a busboy in a restaurant.

CURRENT JOB: Air traffic manager for Denver International Airport, one of the busiest airports in the world.

BEEN THERE, DONE THAT

Gregory Mueller has devoted more than 30 years to his work with the Federal Aviation Administration. During his career, he has worked in many different places as an air traffic controller or manager. He spent much of his time in the midwest, including six years at Chicago's O'Hare Airport. O'Hare is a busy intersection for airplanes, so he got lots of experience there! He also spent some time in California and then headed back to Denver.

In the past three decades, he has watched the technology change and improve the way controllers handle air traffic. He has frequently updated his skills by learning how to use new, state-of-the-art equipment and appreciates how it has made his job easier as well as making air travel safer for planes and people. On the horizon, he's looking forward to even better technology and the improvements they will bring.

NEVER A DULL MOMENT

One of the most challenging jobs he's ever had is his present one as the air traffic manager at Denver's new airport. Three years before the airport even opened, he was on the job, planning and getting ready. He wanted to be sure that things went smoothly when planes began to take off and land at the new facility.

This meant testing procedures and equipment. It meant being there for airplanes that wanted to land to check the facility out. It meant hiring new people and getting them trained. It meant lots of coordination with local officials and administrators. Closing down the old airport, working with others to be sure that the new one opened on time, and making sure everything was operating correctly were major tasks.

Now that the new airport is up and running, Mueller oversees all the activities of the tower and is responsible for the safety of all the planes in the air around the airport and as they take off and land.

A GOOD CONTROLLER

Mueller says that one of the most important skills of a good controller is the ability to think fast—even with lots of distractions! He must be able to do many things at once. He must also be able to visualize the relationships of planes in the air just by looking at a little radar screen.

He's found that the only way to be ready to handle all this mentally is to be in top physical shape. Mueller works out regularly to keep at his best. A good workout also helps to relieve the stress that comes with the job.

WORLDWIDE CONNECTIONS

Controllers talk to one another as they pass the responsibility for an aircraft over to the next person. Each is a link in an intricate worldwide system of controllers and equipment. Mueller says it's fun to be part of that system and to know that you are "in touch" with others around the world who are doing the same thing.

Broadcaster

SKILL SET

- ✔ TALKING
- ✔ COMPUTERS
- ✔ WRITING

SHORTCUTS

GO visit a radio station in your area.

READ *You've Got to Be Believed* by Bert Decker (New York: St. Martin's Press, 1992).

TRY interviewing a friend about their favorite sport.

WHAT IS A BROADCASTER?

Broadcasters, also known as disk jockeys (DJ's for short), radio announcers, newscasters, or just plain announcers, spend their time talking into a radio or television microphone. Depending on their designated roles, broadcasters might make announcements, read advertisements, or present the news. They scope out the weather and special events for listeners.

Whatever the forum, their job consists of three parts: to inform, entertain, and keep things on track. It can be quite a juggling act. The music or TV programs, the commercials, the news, and the broadcaster's comments have to be synchronized to fit within a very specific timeframe. It's the broadcaster's job to keep things running along without a hitch (such as embarrassing dead airtime or rambling dialogues). It takes total concentration to keep every second of airtime on track.

It isn't easy, but when someone tunes into their radio or television show, it has to sound and look as though it is.

Broadcasters working on live radio or television shows must be prepared to work crazy hours. A DJ hosting a morning show may have to be ready to hit the airwaves as early as 4 or 5 A.M. to reach the early rush-hour audience. Sometimes traffic reporters will work the morning rush hour and then come back for the evening rush hour. In addition, they prepare their reports, get information, do interviews, set up programs, and keep in touch with their listeners. It can make for a very long day.

Talk show hosts interview a wide variety of guests during either live or prerecorded segments. The show might be about a specific subject, about a guest's life, or about a timely topic. Talk show hosts rarely improvise when they do a show, even though the goal is often to sound as if they are engaged in a comfortable conversation with a good friend. They spend lots of time doing homework, learning as much as possible about the guest they will be talking with and the subject they will be discussing. Reading, researching, planning, and practice are regular features of the job.

Successful broadcasters of all varieties share some common traits, including

- a distinctive voice and great diction
- exceptional public speaking skills
- the ability to think on their feet
- strong people skills and empathy for others' concerns and opinions
- the curiosity to stay informed about current events

To become a broadcaster, a well-rounded education and a base of experience is generally required. Bachelor's degrees with a major in subjects such as journalism, English, communications, mass media, broadcasting, or liberal arts are good choices. Experience typically starts working behind the scenes at a radio or television station. It is not at all unusual for broadcasters to get their start in smaller towns and cities and work their way up to the major "markets."

For someone with something to say, broadcasting can be an especially rewarding career choice.

TRY IT OUT

HOST YOUR OWN SHOW

Take a tape recorder and do your own show. Arrange a time to interview one of your teachers (or maybe even your school principal). Before your scheduled meeting, learn as much as you can about the person and the issues you want to talk about (in other words, do your homework first). List your questions and stick to a reasonable time limit by keeping the conversation focused.

Once it's recorded, play it for your friends or your parents. Ask them to compare your interview to a radio show they often listen to.

SAME SONG, DIFFERENT VERSE

Take this idea a little further by making up an entire radio show. Put together 15 or 30 minutes (to the second!) of music, ads, and talk. Make it sound as though you are hosting a show on your favorite radio station. Then, the next time your friends are over, pop it into your cassette player and see if you can fool them into thinking you really did a special guest broadcast.

VIEWS FROM THE STREET

With your trusty microphone and tape recorder handy, stand in the cafeteria during lunch hour. Ask a variety of students for their opinions about a hot issue currently being discussed at your school. For instance, ask what they think about a new rule, if they like the new lunch menu, or how they'd feel about going to school year-round. Another good opportunity for interviews is right after one of the sports teams has had a big win (or a big loss). Make sure to be prepared with questions before you start interviewing people.

TURN ON AND TUNE IN

For this activity, you'll need a computer and a television set. First, tune in to CNN, a major 24-hour news channel, at the beginning of any hour for the day's headline news. Listen carefully and take notes about major stories that they cover.

Next, go to CNN's Internet website (http://www.cnn.com). Read the reports about each of the major stories covered on television. Identify the main points in each article and check your notes to see which ones where covered on the telecast. Compare the similarities and differences between a live report and a written one.

MAY I HAVE YOUR ATTENTION, PLEASE

Most schools have a public address system that's used to make announcements to the entire school. Volunteer to be an official school announcer. Practice your lines before turning on the microphone and look for ways to spice things up a bit, for example with music or humor. This can be an excellent first step toward a broadcasting career. And, you'll have a built-in audience.

CHECK IT OUT

American Federation of Television and Radio Artists
260 Madison Avenue
New York, New York 10016

Broadcast Education Association
1771 N Street NW
Washington, D.C. 20036

National Association of Broadcasters
1771 N Street NW
Washington, D.C. 20036

Radio and Television News Directors Association
1717 K Street NW, Suite 615
Washington, D.C. 20006

GET ACQUAINTED

Laura Woloch, Talk Show Host

CAREER PATH

CHILDHOOD ASPIRATION: To be a dancer or performer.

FIRST JOB: At age 10, she started a lawn mowing company with her two brothers.

CURRENT JOB: Professional trainer and radio talk show host.

A LITTLE HOUSE INSPIRATION

All her life, Laura Woloch enjoyed the "Little House" books. Laura Ingalls Wilder's tales inspired her to take on the pioneering spirit and keep things simple in her life. Her weekly show is full of hints about how businesses can simplify and be more productive too.

NETWORKING FOR GUESTS

Woloch spends lots of her time getting to know people who might make interesting guests on her show. She might meet them at a party, on an airplane, at the grocery store, or at a school event. Sometimes she finds them on the Internet and chats with them by e-mail before they ever do the show with her. She looks for people who have a story to tell or for experts who have something new to share.

Most of the people on her show don't travel a very long distance. That is the case with many radio stations. Exceptions occur when a talk show host has out-of-town guests (such as a theater troupe or music group) who are in town to do another show and need to promote it on the radio.

IT CAN BE LONELY

Sometimes it can be lonely doing a talk show. Woloch says she misses the immediate feedback of an audience. If she tells a joke, there's no one to laugh at it. It's also hard to come up with fresh, new material each week. When she leaves it up to the guest, it usually comes out all right, but when she has to think of a new way to talk about a subject she's covered plenty of times before, it's tough.

LISTEN, LISTEN, LISTEN

The most important part of her job is listening. Woloch says she must listen carefully to what the guest is saying. She can't be thinking about what she's going to fix for dinner or who she's going to have on the next show. She has to concentrate on this show, this guest, and this subject. She calls it "living in the moment."

She also has to think on her feet. What she says *always* has to make sense. And she must remember that she's *live*. There's no chance to say, "I don't like what I just said, can we back the tape up and re-record it?"

COMPUTERS RULE

Computers rule the roost on her show. All sessions are done with the help of computerized equipment. The computer allows her to make a recording of the show and replay it later. This helps her pinpoint mistakes, and highlight the things she did well. Woloch has to know how all the equipment works, since the engineer isn't always around to fix things.

LOUIE THE LAWYER

In Woloch's opinion, her most interesting guest was Louie the Lawyer. The show was all about ethics and how to keep companies out of trouble. She found it fascinating to explore values and principles with an attorney. At first she thought, "Ethical lawyer? Can't be!" She soon found out differently and had fun doing the show.

LOVES TO TALK

Woloch loves to talk. She also loves to listen. Doing the talk show gives her the opportunity to meet new people and make lots of friends. She also learns a lot about all sorts of things. Her advice to you? Enjoy it!

Corporate Trainer

SKILL SET

- ✔ BUSINESS
- ✔ TALKING
- ✔ WRITING

SHORTCUTS

GO get involved in your school's debate team.

READ the business section of the local newspaper, the *Wall Street Journal*, and business magazines such as *Working Woman* and *Entrepreneur* to find out what businesspeople are talking about.

TRY teaching one of your friends how to do something they have never done before.

WHAT IS A CORPORATE TRAINER?

Corporate trainers are to the business world what school teachers are to your world. They are the people who teach, train, inform, motivate, and educate businesspeople on topics ranging from business etiquette to the latest computer technology.

To succeed in this specialized area of adult education, a corporate trainer must be a team builder, a public speaker, and a good listener. He or she must be comfortable speaking in front of both large and small groups of businesspeople and must possess the presentation skills necessary to get and keep the attention of his or her audience.

Training business professionals is quite different from teaching children. The "students" come with much more experience and higher expectations, and quite often they have paid a significant amount of money to be there. The corporate trainer's job is to value their experience, meet their expectations, and give them their money's worth.

Corporate trainers generally must become experts in at least three areas, including

- Communication skills. Remember, successful communication involves both giving and receiving information. Corporate trainers must be skilled in giving public presentations and in receiving student feedback.

- Business skills. In order to train others, a corporate trainer has to know something that others want to learn. Whether it's marketing, technology, or personal development skills, the trainer has to know all there is to know about their topic.
- Adult education skills. Knowing what techniques work best with a professional audience is key to a successful training session.

A good corporate trainer or public speaker can motivate his or her audience to feel better about themselves and their abilities. The trainer encourages the audience to think in a whole different way, to look at a problem from a new angle, or to test out fresh skills.

As is true for many careers, there are quite a few routes to becoming a corporate trainer. Some corporate trainers begin their careers as teachers, and some get their start working within the human resources system of a larger company, while others are very experienced professionals who have accumulated a lot of information to share with others. Corporate trainers can work as the employees of a corporation or may offer their services to any number of clients as private consultants.

Preparing to become a corporate trainer is varied. Because the profession often involves interfacing with a well-educated audience, a strong educational background is important. This can take the form of degrees in education, business, communication, or any number of specialized areas. Experience is also an important part of building credibility as a trainer.

In our world's ever-changing workplace, keeping up with the latest skills, technology, and information is necessary for survival in business. Corporate trainers play a big role in keeping the workforce ready and able to tackle new challenges.

TRY IT OUT

SHOW AND TELL

Pick a subject you want to learn more about. Go to the library and find out all you can about that subject. Develop three to five key points you want to communicate. Put these together as the basis for a short training session of your own. Find ways to include interesting stories and visual aids to help make your key points and keep everyone's interest.

Gather your family or a group of your friends together and make the presentation. Leave time for your audience to ask questions and discuss their interest in the subject. At the end, ask for feedback on your presentation style.

BUILD A BETTER SANDWICH

Gather several friends together in your kitchen. Show them how to make your favorite sandwich. Be sure you take it step by step. Build it up and make it great! Find out if everyone else likes it as much as you do. If they don't, find out what they would do to improve it.

TAKE OVER FOR YOUR TEACHER

Talk to one of your teachers. Volunteer to teach part of a class. Spend lots of time preparing. Be sure you know everything you can about the subject you will teach. Get some feedback and comments from your teacher about how you did. Talk to your classmates. How did they feel about your "training job"? How do you feel about any negative comments from your friends?

THE TOAST OF THE TALK

Toastmasters International is an organization that consists of about 8,000 clubs all over the world. These clubs get together to help each other improve their public speaking skills. It's a great source of high-quality, low-cost communication training. While the main clubs are only available to people who are 18 and older, Toastmasters also provides great resources for youth leadership clubs.

If there isn't already a club up and running in your area, you'll have to find a local club or adult willing to sponsor a new club. Call Toastmasters (800-993-7732) to find out what's available in your area.

TALK YOUR WAY TO SUCCESS

No matter what you end up doing in life, good communication skills will be vital to your success. *Teenagers Preparing for the Real World: A Formula for Success* by Chad Foster (Lithonia, Ga.: Rising Books, 1995) is an excellent resource, with several ideas for building these skills.

CHECK IT OUT

American Society for Training and Development
1640 King Street
Box 1443
Alexandria, Virginia 22313

National Association of Workforce Development Professionals
1620 I Street NW, Suite LL30
Washington, D.C. 20006-4005

National Speakers Association
1500 South Priest Drive
Tempe, Arizona 85281
http://www.nsaspeaker.org

Toastmasters International
P.O. Box 9052
Mission Viejo, California 92690

GET ACQUAINTED

Jerome Jewell, Corporate Trainer

CAREER PATH

CHILDHOOD ASPIRATION: To be an architect or jet pilot.

FIRST JOB: Mowing lawns one summer in Queens, New York.

CURRENT JOB: President of his own consulting company, Jewell Consulting Group.

GONE FISHING

"Give someone a fish, and you feed him for a day. Teach someone how to fish, and you feed him for a lifetime." As a corporate trainer, Jerome Jewell feels he is teaching employees how to fish.

Jewell worked his way up in a very large corporation. When he first was put in a leadership position, he found that giving employees some training helped them develop as individuals. This, in turn, made them better employees. As he got more involved in training people, he discovered he really liked it—and was good at it. He also discovered that the key to effective training was not telling someone what to do or how to act but helping them learn how to think about their jobs.

He now spends most of his time training employees for big companies. He helps them figure out how to be more productive and to work together with others for better results. He does this all over the world.

DIFFERENT CULTURES

Have you ever wondered what would happen if you got 10 people together and asked them to agree about how to do something? If each of those 10 people came from a different country, with a different cultural background, speaking a different language, it might be hard to get them to agree on anything.

Jewell works with this type of situation often. He finds it fascinating to watch the interaction between people when they are trying to figure out a problem. A person from Mexico will think differently about things than a person from Germany. They have different ideas because they have different experiences. If there isn't a common language between them, it will be harder for them to communicate. But Jewell makes it happen.

LIGHTBULBS

When his students find the solution to the problem, he says it's like turning a light on in a dark room. When this happens, he knows that the changes being made are long lasting. This is Jewell's favorite part of his job.

Often he will have a former student call him and say: "You really changed my life. Thank you. Here's what happened to me." He loves hearing their success stories.

He remembers having a woman come up to him after one class. She was in tears when she told him she had just been promoted to supervisor in a large organization. It seemed that everyone except her was convinced that she had what it would take to be successful. All her friends and coworkers urged her to "go for it!" She didn't think she could. Jewell asked the right questions and helped her to see for herself that she had the ability to make it.

LISTEN. DON'T TALK

A corporate trainer must be a good listener. Jewell says that a corporate trainer must like to listen almost more than he or she likes to talk. A good trainer will help students find their own solutions. This is achieved by asking questions and guiding people in their search, not by telling them right away what the answer is.

This takes a lot of self-discipline. It also helps to recognize that teachers and trainers learn from their students as much as their students learn from them.

IF AT FIRST YOU DON'T SUCCEED . . .

You may have to try out a lot of possibilities before you find the best approach. When Jewell had his first job cutting grass in the summer, he had lots of people telling him how to trim the lawn. Everyone had a different idea.

Some of those early trainers would demonstrate the "right way" for a few feet, and then he would have to finish the rest. Others would simply try to tell him the right way. He found out that in order to really learn it, he had to do it himself. A learning-while-earning approach is one that he heartily recommends.

HIS ADVICE TO YOU

Don't become a corporate trainer because you think you will make lots of money. Do it because you love to help people improve themselves. The money will follow. It can be draining emotionally, but if you go into it with your whole heart, it can be richly rewarding far beyond any money you will be paid.

Flight Attendant

SKILL SET

- ✔ TALKING
- ✔ TRAVEL
- ✔ SCIENCE

SHORTCUTS

GO take a tour of the airport nearest you.

READ *Things That Go Bump in the Flight* by Captain Robert Welch (Cincinnati, Ohio: Betterway Publications, 1987).

TRY serving a meal in a nursing home nearby.

WHAT IS A FLIGHT ATTENDANT?

Flight attendants have two priorities. The first, and most important, is to be sure the passengers and crew on board an aircraft are safe. The second is to make the flight as comfortable and pleasant an experience as possible. This is where the beverages, smiles, and onboard movies come in handy.

The main reason flight attendants are on board is to ensure that the safety regulations of the Federal Aviation Administration (FAA) are followed. If an emergency arises during a flight, flight attendants must be prepared to handle it. They must be ready to open emergency exits, be sure oxygen is available if needed, check to be sure seat belts are securely fastened, and help passengers with their life jackets or get out quickly in a crisis. They also have to be ready to give first aid if someone gets sick while the plane is in the air.

When the flight attendants are not involved in seeing to the safety of the passengers, they are seeing to their comfort. This includes serving beverages and meals. This process involves pushing 200-pound beverage and meal carts up and down a very narrow aisle and using every people-pleasing skill they possess to keep a planeload of passengers satisfied.

Meals might be anything from a bag of peanuts and a beverage to a seven-course meal on an international flight in the first-class section. The flight attendant may have to prepare it, heat it up, or just unwrap it, depending on the type of food served.

Meals aren't the only service-oriented task that a flight attendant must take care of. There are the children flying without a supervising adult to keep an eye on. The passengers with special needs such as dietary restrictions and physical disabilities must be accommodated. Then, of course, there is the hard-to-please passenger who keeps things interesting. Keeping track of everyone's needs requires diplomacy, tact, and great communication skills.

Before takeoff, the flight attendants are briefed on special problems and possible weather conditions along the route that might make the flight bumpy or hazardous. They also must check to be sure that the safety equipment aboard the aircraft is in working order and ready at a moment's notice. In addition, they ensure that the cabin is clean and neat, meals and beverages are ready, and headsets and the public

address system are working and that plenty of newspapers and magazines are on hand for the passengers to read.

Flight attendants work different schedules depending on the airline. They may work three to four days and have the rest of the week off. Their flying time each day is limited and they must have a specific amount of break time in between trips (among other rules), so they can be alert and ready to keep passengers safe. With so many flights going to so many different places in the world, scheduling can get pretty tricky.

Flight attendants must be prepared to go anywhere at a moment's notice. Can you imagine being ready to fly to Alaska, getting to the airport, and having the airline tell you that they really need you to fly to Florida instead? So much for the sweaters in your suitcase.

While flight attendants don't have to have a college degree, they have to meet specific requirements and get lots of training from the airline before they start flying. They do this in a simulated plane environment. It looks and acts just like the real thing but doesn't have real passengers. The practice "plane" is actually a tin tube at ground level, not 35,000 feet. Much of the training process covers the many different kinds of emergencies that could occur and what to do about them if they do. Learning a second language provides an extra edge for getting hired and for working the more prestigious international flights.

TRY IT OUT

CONFLICT RESOLUTION

The next time you have friends over to visit, try this activity. Gather about 25 different household items (or just write the names of different items on index cards), such as a tent, a flashlight, a solar battery, a book, etc.—be creative. Tell them that they have just been chosen to take a group trip to the moon, and they may take 10 of these items with them. The tricky part is that everyone has to agree on which items go and which ones stay. Your role is to act as mediator. Use the best diplomatic skills you can muster to bring the group to an agreement.

SPECIAL PEOPLE

Spending time volunteering with special-needs people can be great preparation for a career caring for the public. It will give you confidence to deal with all kinds of people in all kinds of situations—great skills for flight attendants.

Contact your local United Way office to find out about volunteer opportunities in your community. Other places that might welcome a willing volunteer include a local child-care program, nursing home, or community outreach program.

TRAVEL THE WORLD

Take an imaginary trip. Pick a place that you would like to go to. Using your library as a "jumping off point," find out all that you can about that place. Visit a travel agency or two to find out if there are any brochures, posters, or other travel information about your chosen destination. Call around to different airlines and find out what the flight schedule and costs would be. Plan an entire itinerary. Compile all the information in a travel journal, and look forward to the day when you make this travel dream come true.

BROADEN YOUR HORIZONS

If there's someone at your school whose native language is not English, ask them to teach you about their language and culture. Try to spend a little time with them each day, learning new words, swapping foods at lunch, and discovering the many things you have in common. Keep track of your progress by using a small notebook to record everything you learn each day.

INTERNET ALTITUDE

You'll find a variety of useful resources on the Internet. Start at the Flight Attendants Resource Center. Here you'll find links to specific resources, information about minimum hiring requirements, and access to the websites for specific airlines. The Internet address is http://www.flightattendants.com.

CHECK IT OUT

Association of Flight Attendants
1275 K Street NW
Washington, D.C. 20005-4006

Flight Attendant Corporation of America
P.O. Box 260803
Littleton, Colorado 80163

Future Aviation Professionals of America
4959 Massachusetts Boulevard
Atlanta, Georgia 30337
800-JET-JOBS

GET ACQUAINTED

Sue Beeson, Flight Attendant

CAREER PATH

CHILDHOOD ASPIRATION: To be a flight attendant.

FIRST JOB: Helped in the kitchen at a summer camp.

CURRENT JOB: Flight attendant for United Airlines.

SAFETY FIRST

As you can guess, safety is Sue Beeson's first priority when working 30,000 feet above the ground. She wants to be sure that the passengers she is responsible for are prepared for emergencies and are safe at all times. The food service and other "customer service" things that she does are fun, but secondary to the job. Those tasks keep her busy during a flight, but they are not the real reason she's there.

As the daughter of an airline pilot, she began to think about being a flight attendant when she was only six. From that point on, she learned all she could about airplanes, aircraft safety, and dealing with passengers. She traveled the world and always kept her dream of being a flight attendant.

SMILE AND KEEP YOUR COOL

Being a flight attendant means keeping your cool. It means doing the not-so-fun jobs, such as dealing with the grouches, and keeping a smile on your face. Beeson says, "You control yourself, not the situation."

When she has an unreasonable passenger she must deal with, she does so with an infinite amount of patience and graciousness. She is a very poised person. She has found that the more together she is, the more sure of who she is inside, and the easier it is to keep her cool and her smile.

Her job is to bring a solution to the problem, not add fuel to the fire. Being gracious in the face of stress isn't always easy, especially high up in the air. But, it's a necessary ability for a flight attendant to have.

A sense of humor helps too. Being able to laugh with someone often takes the edge off a serious situation. It also helps to keep passengers in a happy mood and makes the plane a fun place to work.

CHANGE IS A CONSTANT

Beeson has been with the airline for more than 20 years. She has lots of seniority. In some jobs, that would mean she'd get the primo assignments. As a flight attendant, because of the nature of the job, she still works holidays and weekends. Her schedule is constantly changing. She must be ready to go anywhere, anytime. She says she's always packed. Could you live out of that little suitcase for two weeks? Beeson loves it!

REFUEL YOURSELF FROM THE PEOPLE AROUND YOU

Beeson sometimes works three to four flights a day and attends to hundreds of people in a very short period of time. She enjoys the people and changes that come with each new flight. Each one is different, because each flight has new faces. She feels invigorated by meeting all these new people and getting to know them. There's an endless variety. She likes to spend some time, when she can, getting to know the people she's taking care of.

On one flight there was a family returning home from Alaska. They had traveled and worked on an environmental research ship for a year and were full of interesting stories about what they had seen and done. On another flight, the plane was full of very important people from Washington, D.C., traveling to Seattle to testify about whether loggers could chop down the trees where the spotted owl lives. Both sides of the argument were on board and talking, talking, talking. She got to hear both sides and watch them begin to come to some agreement about the issues.

OPEN YOUR HORIZONS

Being a flight attendant is what you make it. You can learn a bunch of new things—about yourself, about others, about your world. It's great when you get to go to a new place and have time to see a little of it. Whether it's visiting a temple in Japan, riding a camel in the Middle East, sipping hot chocolate at a sidewalk café in Paris, sailing a boat in New Zealand, or watching a lion chase a gazelle in Africa, your horizon is unlimited.

Hotel Manager

SKILL SET

- ✔ BUSINESS
- ✔ TALKING
- ✔ TRAVEL

SHORTCUTS

GO visit different kinds of hotels, inns, and restaurants in town.

READ all about the special things to see and do in your town.

TRY volunteering at your local chamber of commerce to give information to visitors about your community.

WHAT IS A HOTEL MANAGER?

Hotel managers have to oversee every detail at the hotel. They manage a large staff of people who divide up the many duties.

All the rooms must be cleaned everyday. Added to that, the guests need to be greeted with a smile, checked into the hotel, and shown to their rooms. Luggage needs to be carried too. If your guests need to know about a good restaurant or special things to see in your town, you and your staff need to have the answers. Business conventions need space for meetings. Organizations need space to hold special events. Families need space to celebrate major occasions such as weddings. And, of course, all those guests will want to be entertained after their work is finished, so they'll be looking for the hotel's swimming pool, exercise room, and night clubs. Hotels, motels, and other hospitality establishments have to be prepared to handle these needs and more as "hosts" to any number of overnight guests.

Hotel accommodations run the gamut from the luxury, world-class hotel to the cozy bed-and-breakfast inn with the following types of accommodations in between.

- conference centers
- convention hotels
- executive suites
- health spas
- hotel and motel chains
- resorts
- roadside inns

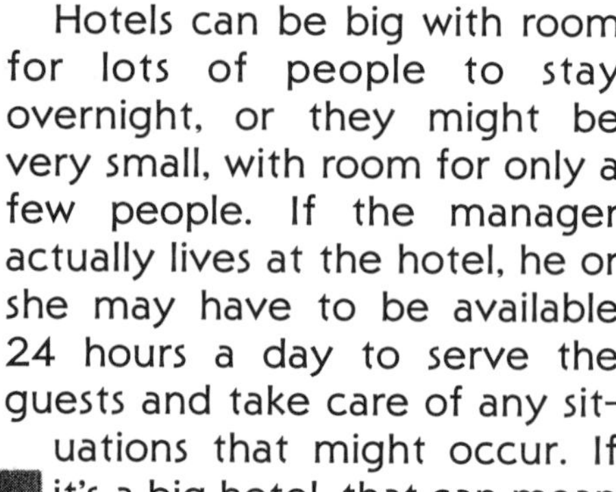

Hotels can be big with room for lots of people to stay overnight, or they might be very small, with room for only a few people. If the manager actually lives at the hotel, he or she may have to be available 24 hours a day to serve the guests and take care of any situations that might occur. If it's a big hotel, that can mean lots of headaches!

The large hotels have people who specialize in taking care of different kinds of problems. Housekeeping will see that the beds are made and the rooms and bathrooms are clean. Maintenance workers will take care of plumbing, electrical, heating, and air-conditioning problems and see that equipment is up-to-date. Groundskeepers will be sure that the grass is cut, the flowers are at their best, and the walks are clean. The front desk will take reservations, check people into the hotel, be sure guests can pay for their rooms, and direct any complaints to the proper department.

In a typical, larger hotel, managers handle specific functions of the operation in areas such as

assistant manager
convention service manager
food services manager
front service manager
general manager
housekeeping manager
reservations manager
resident manager

Small hotels are sometimes called motels, inns, or bed-and-breakfasts. With a very small inn, the owner may be handling all the different tasks by him- or herself.

At a bed-and-breakfast inn (B&B), people spend the night and have breakfast in the morning. In this type of hotel, very often the owner will cook breakfast, clean the rooms and the bathrooms, change the beds, check people in, take reservations, take care of repairs, tell people about special places to visit, and recommend restaurants. It's lots of work, but owners have the chance to meet many people and talk with them.

Dealing with lots of different people is part of every hotel manager's job. Sometimes these people are happy with the service you provide. Sometimes they are not. Strong communications skills, diplomacy, stamina, and lots of charm are valuable assets for hotel managers.

Training requirements for hotel/motel managers vary almost as much as the many types of places where people can spend the night. Some smaller hotels and chains require only high school graduation or an associate's degree in a hospitality-related field. Count on the major chains and more service-oriented places to require more education—a bachelor's in hospitality management for assistant managers and graduate work in hotel administration or business management for general managers. In addition, many hotel corporations offer in-house training opportunities to its management staff.

TRY IT OUT

HAVE A B&B SLEEPOVER

If you have the room at your house, and if your parents say it's OK, have a B&B sleepover. Prepare "rooms" (even if it's just a separate space with a sleeping bag). Place a mint on the pillows. Add any special touches your brain can think of and your budget can afford—potpourri, cute little soaps, magazines, a water bottle, and other comforts are safe bets.

Invite a few friends and have them arrive just after dinner. Provide a snack (fresh, warm cookies are great, or maybe popcorn). Have a fun activity organized. Some suggestions: play a game (charades might be fun), watch a movie, do a puzzle, or whatever you think your guests would enjoy. Use your imagination for this part.

In the morning, have hot chocolate ready for a "wake-up" drink. Fix your guests a nice breakfast. Help them gather up their possessions before they leave, and see them off with a smile. But, remember, once the guests are gone, some of your work is just beginning. Be sure to "change the sheets," clean the bathrooms, and return your house back to normal.

LET YOUR FINGERS DO THE WALKING

Use the yellow pages for your area and find the section for hotels/motels. Make a list of all the larger chains that have toll-free numbers. Call each hotel and ask them to send you a brochure that describes their accommodations and services.

Next, make a list of the best feature of each hotel. When you are finished, rank the top three places where you'd like to spend the night.

BED-AND-BREAKFAST INTERNSHIP

Some bed-and-breakfasts will let young people work there for a short period of time. Arrange to shadow the innkeeper for a day. Ask for the opportunity to try different tasks. Try making all the beds one day and helping out in the kitchen the next. Do everything you can to get a sense of how the whole operation runs day to day.

Do a good job. At the very least, you'll provide some much-needed relief for a busy innkeeper. And, you might even work yourself into a part-time job.

BREAKFAST TRYOUTS

Try making breakfast for your family every morning for a week. Plan your menus and make sure you have all the ingredients on hand. Set the table the night before so that you can add some nice touches—flowers, fancy napkins, and other touches can help get the day off to a good start.

TAKE A TOUR

Pick a hotel or inn close to where you live. Ask the owner or manager to give you a tour. Find out how the hotel works. Better yet, if you are traveling with your parents, see if you can

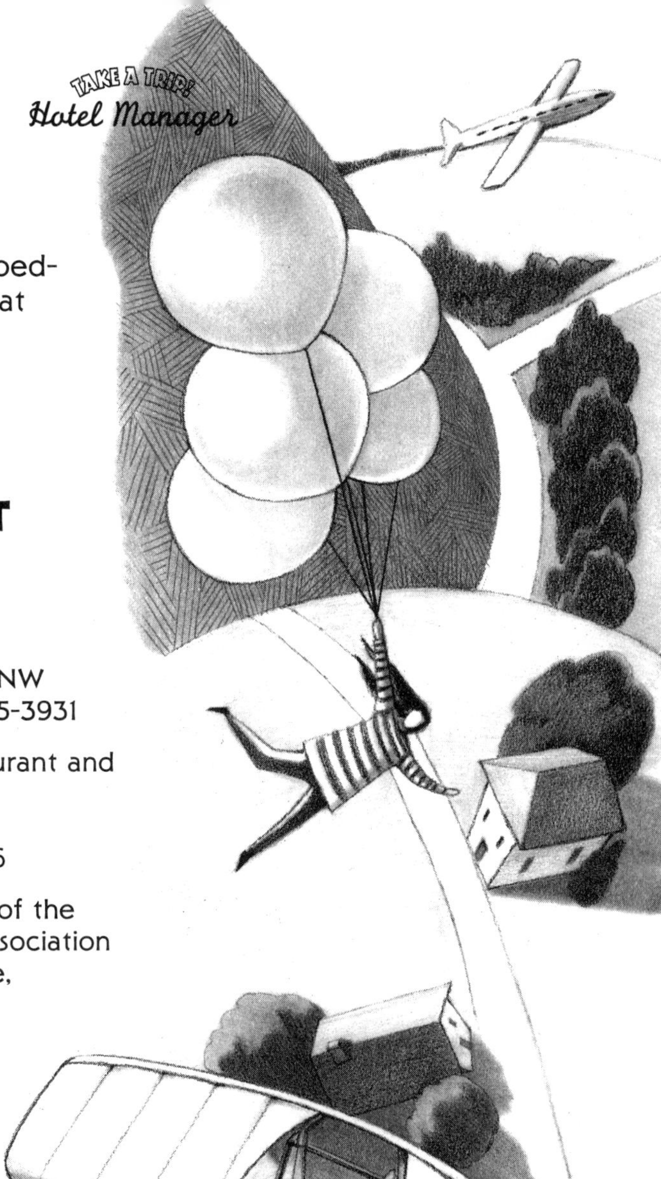

stay in a small inn or bed-and-breakfast. See what you think of the B&B experience firsthand.

CHECK IT OUT

American Hotel and
Motel Association
Information Center
1201 New York Avenue NW
Washington, D.C. 20005-3931

Council on Hotel, Restaurant and
Institutional Education
1200 17th Street NW
Washington, D.C. 20036

Educational Foundation of the
National Restaurant Association
250 South Wacker Drive,
Suite 1400
Chicago, Illinois 60606

Educational Institute of
the American Hotel
and Motel Association
888 Seventh Avenue
New York, New York 10106

National Executive Housekeepers
Association, Inc.
1001 Eastwind Drive, Suite 301
Westerville, Ohio 43081
800-200-6342

Professional Association of
Innkeepers International
P.O. Box 90710
Santa Barbara, California 93190
http://www.paii.org

GET ACQUAINTED

Julie Mordecai, Innkeeper

CAREER PATH

CHILDHOOD ASPIRATION: To find a way to see the world and learn new things.

FIRST JOB: Baby-sitting.

CURRENT JOB: Proprietor of the Cottonwood Inn, a small bed-and-breakfast inn in southern Colorado.

EVERYONE SAID SHE WAS CRAZY

At first, owning the Cottonwood Inn was a way to pay the mortgage on the house Mordecai and her husband had bought. As it became increasingly profitable, it turned into a full-time business. All her friends said she was crazy and that she wouldn't last a year.

At first, the inn had three rooms, all of which shared a bath. Mordecai has remodeled and added more bedrooms and bathrooms and a large commercial kitchen in which she cooks breakfast every morning.

She lasted, and the business took off. It was scary, but she did it. And it is lots of hard work, but the chance to meet lots of different people makes up for it.

EXPERIENCE COUNTS

Mordecai found that planning how she was going to be successful helped. She had worked in large hotels, so she had some experience in making people comfortable. As she began the inn, she took some business courses to help her do her budgeting and marketing. Things began to take shape, and she found her business steadily growing.

WEARING MANY HATS

At first, Mordecai was doing everything herself (with husband George's help). She got up every morning at 5:00 to make scrumptious breakfasts for her guests. She then made beds, cleaned rooms, and scrubbed bathrooms until the house was spotless. She worked on the computer keeping her records up, took reservations for future nights, and planned the breakfast menu for the following day.

Each evening she greeted guests as they checked in, helped them with their luggage, and acted as a self-appointed local tour director when necessary. Often she made dinner reservations for her guests or recommended places to go and things to do in her local community. (She even knows where to find some of the best fishing spots!)

THE EXTRA TOUCHES COUNT

Each room in the inn is decorated with different themes and color schemes. Bathrooms all have bubble bath available and deep tubs in which to relax. Beds are extra comfortable. Each evening guests are greeted with fresh, warm, homemade cookies. This attention to the little details makes people feel comfortable away from home and guarantees that travelers return time after time.

SUCCESS HAS ITS PERKS

Now Mordecai is busy almost all year accommodating people who fill her house with laughter and conversation. She continues to do many of the things she has always done but has now hired others to help with some of the jobs.

The help frees up time for her to do other things she's always wanted to do, such as write a breakfast cookbook. She has an assistant chef who loves to cook and helps her in the kitchen in the mornings. With both of them coming up with new things to fix for breakfast, the menus are incredibly scrumptious.

Law Enforcement Officer

SKILL SET

- ✔ ADVENTURE
- ✔ SPORTS
- ✔ TALKING

SHORTCUTS

GO ride with a police officer on patrol. Call your local police department to ask if they have a ride-along program.

READ any Sherlock Holmes mystery by Sir Arthur Conan Doyle or any of the Miss Marple stories by Agatha Christie.

TRY volunteering as a crossing guard or hall monitor for your school.

WHAT IS A LAW ENFORCEMENT OFFICER?

There are lots of shows on television about police officers and detectives. You've probably watched some and may think you have a pretty good idea about what a law enforcement officer does. But it isn't all action adventure. You sure don't catch the bad guys in a nice, tidy hour; sometimes you never get them.

Law enforcement officers include police officers, detectives, and sheriffs. The field might also include special agents working for the Federal Bureau of Investigation, the Drug Enforcement Administration, the Border Patrol, or the U.S. Marshals Service. All of these people are responsible for enforcing different kinds of laws and have different kinds of responsibilities.

In a typical day, a police officer in a smaller community might be called upon to do lots of different things such as direct traffic, patrol a beat, calm a family fight, make an arrest, pick up a barking dog, or collect evidence to be used in court. He or she might also be asked to testify in court about an arrest or talk to young people in a school or elderly people in a nursing home. Police officers deal with people from many different walks of life—some very rich and some very poor, some educated and some illiterate. They wear lots of hats and do lots of jobs.

In a larger city, a police officer might specialize in a particular area such as chemical analysis, fingerprint identification, polygraph operation, or handwriting analysis. On the beat, he or she might ride a horse, a bicycle, or a motorcycle as a "mounted patrol." He or she might have a dog to work with as part of the canine corps and spend time looking for drugs or tracking kidnap victims. Some cities have special emergency response teams that are assigned to deal with certain types of problems, such as terrorism, snipers, burglary, vice, or drugs.

A special agent working for the government might guard the president of the United States or investigate a bombing or the illegal production or sale of alcohol or firearms. Other possible tasks could include enforcing the laws that prevent smugglers from bringing illegal items into this country, or tracking down some counterfeit money. Some special agents investigate people who cheat on their taxes, while others search for bank robbers and members of organized crime. Others specialize in background checks, determining if a person is trustworthy enough to work in a top security job.

To become a law enforcement officer, you must be at least 20 years old, be a U.S. citizen, and have a valid driver's license.

You must pass certain written tests as well as some basic physical ones for vision, hearing, and drug use. After passing those entrance hurdles, you must meet some fairly rigorous physical standards of endurance, strength, and agility. Needless to say, you have to clean record—free from any trouble and criminal activity—to even be considered as a law enforcement officer.

Most local police departments require at least a high school education. If you want to work as a special agent for the federal government, you may need a college degree in any number of subject areas. Find out what the specific requirements are for the specific type of law enforcement you hope to pursue.

TRY IT OUT

EXPLORE YOUR OPTIONS

Many police departments have an explorer program or cadet program just for young people. Explorers get uniforms, go through a special police academy, and ride along with police officers. Call your local police department to find out if this is available and how you can sign up.

CURL UP WITH A GOOD MYSTERY

Borrow a stack of mystery books from the library. You can't go wrong with the Sherlock Holmes classics or anything by Agatha Christie, but ask the librarian for other suggestions.

While you are reading, keep track of all the clues and your own suspicions in a notebook. Before you read the concluding chapter, piece together all the clues and write down the name of the guilty party. Finish reading the book to find out if you were right.

WHO DUNNIT?

Besides the traditional mystery stories, there are a number of fun products to put your investigative skills to the test. Try

- Be Puzzled: Inspector Cross Mystery Jigsaw Puzzle Thrillers by Henry Slesar (Bloomfield, Conn.: Lombard

Marketing, 1992). Put the 1,000-piece puzzle together and solve the mystery.

- *Five Minute Mysteries* by Don Wulffson (Los Angeles: Lowell House Juvenile, 1994). This book contains 37 challenging cases of murder and mayhem.
- 3D Mystery Jigsaw Puzzle (Buffalo, N.Y.: Buffalo Games, 1993). There are millions of possibilities but only one way to solve the crime that occurred in this three-dimensional building.

You should be able to find these products, or products like them, at your local bookstore. If you can't, order by phone (with a parent and credit card handy) from one of the world's largest bookstores: the Tattered Cover. Call 800-833-9327. Or order on-line at http://www.amazon.com.

TRAFFIC COP

Make an appointment to talk with an officer at your local police station. Ask what kinds of things get drivers into trouble most often. Is it speeding? Parking? Failure to yield?

As you ride in the car with your parents, see if you observe any of these violations. Keep a notebook handy and record license plate numbers, location, time, and car type. At the end of a month, add up your numbers to find out how many tickets you could have issued if you'd been in uniform.

CHECK IT OUT

Academy of Criminal Justice Sciences: Secretariat
North Kentucky University
402 Nunn Hall
Nunn Drive
Highland Heights, Kentucky 41099-5998

American Federation of Police
1000 Connecticut Avenue NW, Suite 9
Washington, D.C. 20036

American Police Academy
Lock Box 15350
Chevy Chase, Maryland 20815

American Society of Criminology
1314 Kinnear Road, Suite 212
Columbus, Ohio 43212

International Association of Chiefs of Police
515 North Washington Street
Alexandria, Virginia 22314-2357

National Council on Crime and Delinquency
1325 G Street NW, Suite 770
Washington, D.C. 20005

National Sheriff's Association
1450 Duke Street
Alexandria, Virginia 22314-3490

GET ACQUAINTED

Carrie Sherr, Police Officer

CAREER PATH

CHILDHOOD ASPIRATION: To be an actress.

FIRST JOB: Delivered newspapers when she was 11.

CURRENT JOB: One of only five women police officers in a police department of 105 sworn-in officers in California.

A DREAM FULFILLED

Carrie Sherr wanted to be an actress; in fact, that's what she focused on in college. It wasn't until she married a deputy sheriff that she realized that law enforcement was what she really wanted to do. She remembered a female D.A.R.E. (Drug Abuse Resistance Education) officer who spoke at her school when she was in the ninth grade. Sherr was impressed with her and with the possibilities for women in law enforcement.

MAKING A DIFFERENCE

For Sherr, the opportunity to make a difference in people's lives is what her job is all about. She remembers arresting two teenage girls for shoplifting. One girl had a prior arrest record. This girl, who wasn't the least bit sorry about what they had done, told Sherr that her friend had done all the stealing.

When Sherr talked with her friend, the second girl broke down into tears. Sherr spent some time talking to her, reminding her that she didn't have to live her life that way and that she could start right then and make a change. Evidently, that arrest and the talk with Sherr changed her life for the better. The second girl eventually wrote a thank-you letter to Sherr's police department.

Sherr says that working with kids, keeping them out of prison and off drugs, is her priority. She really wants to make a difference with young people.

MIRROR IMAGE

Sometimes being a police officer is similar to being a mirror. If Sherr stops someone and the person is belligerent and unkind, expecting that she will be too, she often finds it necessary to be extra firm. If someone treats her with respect and kindness, she mirrors that, making the "run in with the law" a more positive experience.

A big part of being a police officer is keeping your cool when everyone else is losing theirs. An even temperament is a definite requirement. It's too easy to mirror the person you're talking to, and that isn't always good.

JUST FOR FUN

Sherr works out twice a day. Since physical fitness is such an important part of her job, she keeps herself in top shape. On any given day she may play racquetball in the morning and then work out in the gym in the evening. It's great for getting rid of the stress that piles up from the job.

ALL IN A DAY'S WORK

For Sherr, her fellow officers are like family. On a typical day she might work more than 12 hours, much of it with the same people.

Part of that time is spent patrolling—just being visible in the neighborhood. Most of her time (more than 70 percent) is spent on "activities": making arrests, pulling people over for traffic violations, stopping family disturbances. Keeping the peace (in other words, telling people to turn down the stereos and control the partying) is another big part of her job.

PAPERWORK GALORE

Sherr's job involves lots of paperwork. Laptops in the patrol cars have helped, but she still spends a lot of her time filling out forms and making reports. Good communication skills are a must. Law enforcement officers not only have to use verbal skills to help solve problems, but they also have to use their writing skills to submit a report about each incident.

SOME GOOD ADVICE

If you want to be a police officer, get involved in sports or other after-school activities. Keep busy. Stay out of trouble and away from drugs and alcohol. Live by the rules, since you'll have to enforce them later.

Minister/Priest/Rabbi

SKILL SET

- ✔ TALKING
- ✔ HISTORY
- ✔ WRITING

SHORTCUTS

GO to your church, synagogue, or other house of worship. If you have never been to a place of worship, pick one close to home, find out when services for young people are held, and attend one.

READ the Bible, the Koran, the Torah, or other holy work from cover to cover.

TRY going with your clergyperson as he or she visits someone in your congregation.

WHAT IS A MINISTER/PRIEST/RABBI?

Clergy are people who tend to the spiritual needs of others. Depending on the religion, clergy are called ministers, priests, rabbis, pastors, or preachers. These people lead religious services; organize worship and places of worship; visit elderly and sick people; and conduct funeral services, weddings, and other special services.

Some of them read from their religion's sacred texts, while others write sermons and then deliver them. At times they may also have to raise money to pay for special projects such as a new building or school, or to help a congregation member who needs assistance.

A big part of the job is counseling people. A clergy member might help a young couple get ready for marriage or work through a divorce. He or she might help someone who is sick or terminally ill. The clergy comfort families when someone dies. Often they just help someone see things in a more spiritual way.

Clergy must have a deep commitment to their own faith and their own spirituality. They must be rock solid in their own belief about who God is and who they are, and they must have a firm desire to build and maintain important relationships with others. In some religions, this might mean that they don't have a traditional family with a spouse and children.

Deeper values and spiritual thinking are absolutely necessary to becoming a member of the clergy. College and special religious training are required for many religions. Check out your place of worship to see what is required.

Sometimes the work of the clergy will extend beyond their own place of worship. Communities of different religions might get together to solve a common problem in the neighborhood. Often a clergy member will travel to other areas around the country to speak at different conferences. This interaction provides a way to discuss issues and beliefs with others, widening the clergy's perspective and influence.

Being a member of the clergy isn't a nine-to-five job. It's often more like a round-the-clock commitment. Emergencies and other human needs simply do not confine themselves to regular business hours. Choosing to become part of the clergy is essentially choosing a way of life.

Practicing what you preach is probably one of the most important and most difficult demands of the job. A big part of the job is to lead a congregation in embracing and living by the moral standards and spiritual values that the religion observes.

Deciding to join the clergy is an intensely personal choice. It's a profession that offers the opportunity to do more good for others than almost any other profession there is. It's not for everyone, but for those who feel drawn to serve in this way, it can be a richly rewarding decision.

TRY IT OUT

TAG ALONG

If you are thinking about becoming a clergy member, learn as much as you can about the profession. Spend time with your own religious leader, as well as with others. Talk with them about their experiences and the demands of the profession. Ask if you can tag along as they perform some of their routine clerical duties—visiting the sick, preparing sermons, and planning worship services. Ask them for advice and counsel as you ponder this important decision.

WRITE A SERMON

Pick a subject or a favorite text from your religion's holy text that has special meaning for young people your age. Use a concordance and other references to find out all you can about what it means. Add your own thoughts to how it can be applied to everyday life.

Organize your discoveries into a sermon format. Show it to someone in the clergy and get his or her feedback on it. Ask if there might be an appropriate time to present your message to the youth group at your place of worship.

REACH OUT AND TOUCH SOMEONE

Ministering to others means more than just preaching to them. It involves a genuine investment in the lives of others. Find ways to make a difference in the lives of people in your community. Here are a few ideas.

- Visit a shut-in. This is someone who can't leave the house because of illness or old age. Help fix a meal, clean the house up a bit, or just chat for a while. Did you make him or her feel better just by being there?
- Get involved. Organize a canned food drive with the kids in your school. Take the cans you collect to a homeless shelter or a battered women's shelter.
- Show you care. Volunteer to play games with children staying in a foster home or orphanage.

SACRED GUIDANCE

Make reading the sacred writings of your religion, and even memorizing portions, a part of your daily routine. The clergy's job is to relay these truths in a way that people can relate to and apply to their own lives. Learn it, live it, and make it real in your own life.

INTERNET CHURCH

With such a diverse number of religions and faiths being practiced, it would be virtually impossible to include them all here in this book. Instead, use your Internet search engine and get in touch with resources throughout the world. Simply type the name of the denomination or religion you want to research (for example, Presbyterian, Catholic, Jewish, Hindu) and get ready for a big response. Discover the role of religions in our world from home or school!

You can narrow down your search specification if necessary, but take time to browse a variety of sources to gain a broader perspective.

CHECK IT OUT

You'll want to find out about associations that are part of your own belief system. Ask your clergy for the names and addresses of these groups. In the meantime, the following groups can provide plenty of opportunities to serve humankind.

American Youth Work Center
1751 N Street NW, Suite 302
Washington, D.C. 20036

Boy Scouts of America
P.O. Box 152079
Riving, Texas 75015-2079

Girl Scouts of the USA National Headquarters
830 Third Avenue
New York, New York 10020
800-223-0624

Salvation Army
799 Bloomfield Avenue
Verona, New Jersey 07044

Volunteers in Service to America
1100 Vermont Avenue NW, Room 8100
Washington, D.C. 20525

Volunteers of America
3813 North Causeway Boulevard
Metairie, Louisiana 70002

Volunteer—The National Center
1111 North 19th Street, Suite 500
Arlington, Virginia 22209

Youth Volunteer Corps
1080 Washington
Kansas City, Missouri 64105-2216

Youth Service America
1319 F Street NW, Suite 900
Washington, D.C. 20004

GET ACQUAINTED

Robert Gelinas, Minister

CAREER PATH

CHILDHOOD ASPIRATION: To be an orthopedic surgeon.

FIRST JOB: Mowing lawns as a boy.

CURRENT JOB: Copastor at the Base Chapel of the Rockies; director of outreach and missions for the First Presbyterian Church of Golden; and director of cross-cultural training for Mile High Ministries in Denver.

A LUCKY BREAK

When Robert Gelinas was in junior high, one of his favorite things to do was run. So when he broke his foot, not once, but twice over the course of a year, he didn't feet so lucky. The first time wasn't so bad. During the first surgery and medical treatment, he beame intrigued with the idea of becoming a doctor. He even started studying Latin to help prepare himself for a medical career.

When he broke the same foot just two months after the first cast came off, however, he really got discouraged. Lying in bed unable to do the one thing he loved most—

run—he found himself in dire need of some comfort. Fortunately for him, he was at his grandmother's house. His grandmother always kept a Bible handy just for times like this. Thumbing through it, he came upon a passage in Proverbs (16:3) that says "Commit what you do to the Lord and you will succeed." He believes that it was at that precise moment that he felt God's call to become a minister.

JUST ONE SMALL PROBLEM

Having spent a lot of time at his neighborhood church with his grandmother, the idea of becoming a minister was not unwelcome; however, the more he thought about what ministers do, the more worried he became. That's because one of the most important things that ministers do is preach sermons and the thought of speaking in front of a crowd of people was pretty scary to Gelinas.

But once he started telling people whose opinions he valued about his desire to become a minister, they all confirmed that it was a good idea. Gelinas took this as a sign that he was on the right track and decided to trust God to take care of his public-speaking phobia. Apparently, his plan worked because although Gelinas confesses that he still gets butterflies in his stomach every time he starts to preach, this fear hasn't stopped him from becoming a very effective public speaker. He says that he's decided that his job is to faithfully explain the Scriptures in a loving way and that God is responsible for the rest.

EVEN MINISTERS HAVE BAD DAYS

Gelinas says that he considers a good day in the ministry to be one in which he has plenty of time to study and prepare his sermons (he spends at least 15 to 20 hours a week doing this). A good day isn't complete without additional time spent encouraging others in their faith and helping them learn how to be a positive influence in the world. Top this off with a little time to dream about the future of his church, and he'd call it a good day.

On the other hand, a bad day is spent smoothing ruffled feathers. Within his congregation, as with any close community, it's impossible not to hurt someome's feelings now and then. Start the day with a people crisis and end it with a batch of paperwork needing immediate attention, and you'll have just the right ingredients for the kind of day that Gelinas dreads.

DIVERSITY IS MORE THAN A BUZZWORD

One of the more unusual aspects of Gelinas' work involves organizing "urban immersion" programs, a fancy term that means bringing people of different races and cultures into the inner city to work on a common project. By living and working together as equals, people get a chance to discover their similarities and dispel some of the stereotypes they might have about different races. The theory behind the program is that the city provides a great training ground for teaching people how to live as Christians. Through this work, Gelinas hopes to teach others how to serve God as He designed them to serve—together as one people.

GO WITH WHAT YOU'VE GOT

Gelinas says that it didn't take long for him to discover what his strengths were as a minister. Teaching and leading are his strong points, so he finds ways to emphasize them in his work. He says that one of the most important things he's learned as a minister is to do what he does well and to give the others in his church a chance to do what they do well. It's a formula that has worked well with his various ministries.

According to Gelinas, it is also good advice for a young person trying to decide what to do with his or her life. Figure out what you do well and go with it!

News Reporter

SKILL SET

- ✔ COMPUTERS
- ✔ TALKING
- ✔ WRITING

SHORTCUTS

GO listen to the news on your local radio or television station.

READ your local newspaper and at least one national paper every day.

TRY reporting the news yourself for your school's radio station or newspaper.

WHAT IS A NEWS REPORTER?

A news reporter works right in the middle of history in the making. Whether it's covering a tornado on the other side of town or a war on the other side of the ocean, reporters stay in the thick of the world's events.

A reporter strives to bring complete, unbiased accounts to his or her audience. A reporter on the trail of a newsworthy story (a "scoop," in industry terms) would find factual details as well as interesting features about the story from a variety of sources. Increasingly, reporters log on the Internet for up-to-the-minute news from around the world. The Internet also provides quick access to an incredible array of research materials. In addition, reporters might use other technological means of securing information quickly by making use of e-mail, a fax machine, or the ever-faithful telephone. They are also privy to news coming in over international wire services.

It is not at all unusual for a story to take reporters out of the office to the very place where the news is taking place. Once there, they get new information by interviewing witnesses or other people associated with the event. They may also be on hand to witness an event and provide eyewitness commentary on a story.

Reporters working for larger newspapers or television stations tend to specialize in a particular area of news such as sports, business, health, religion, politics, schools, crime, or consumer issues. These specialties are often referred to as "beats."

Reporters working for a smaller paper or station may be required to cover more than one "beat."

Within the broadcast journalism field (strictly TV or radio), specific jobs include

anchor, who actually delivers the news on radio or television

investigative reporter, who tracks down the stories behind the headlines

correspondent, who reports from both foreign countries and major U.S. cities such as Washington, D.C.

general assignment reporter, who covers all kinds of stories, whenever and wherever they occur

Most reporters have a college degree specializing in journalism or communications. You can start preparing for a career in journalism now by taking courses in English, journalism, and social studies.

Experience is key to getting your foot in the door at any paper or station—large or small. Most large papers or stations want to see evidence of success at a smaller paper or station, and most smaller papers or stations want to see evidence of journalistic involvement in high school and college. So, experience with the yearbook, school newspaper, or community newspaper is a good start.

TRY IT OUT

MAKE A TAPE

Check your community's paper for the important news. Pick the top stories and work them into a five-minute newscast. Tape it and play it back for your family or friends. If you have access to a video recorder, ask a friend to videotape your newscast.

NETNEWS

Nothing beats the news coverage on the Internet. It's quick, it's thorough, and you have to read only what you want to know about. Go on-line and visit the websites of the following major news stations:

- http://www.abc.com
- http://www.cbs.com
- http://www.cnn.com
- http://www.nbc.com

While you are there, pick one major story from the day's headline news. Compare the way each of these stations covers the story. Look for significant details that are included in one paper but aren't in another. Jot down the three main points of each story and pick out the various angles that each story emphasizes.

TAKE A TOUR

Call your local television news stations and ask if you can arrange for a tour of the facilities. Tell them that you are considering a career in journalism and want to see what it's really like to work at a TV station. With a little luck, you'll get the chance to see the equipment, the sound stage, and even an actual live newscast. With a little more luck, you may get the chance to talk with the reporters.

Be prepared! Have your questions and notepad ready.

PLAY THE NEWS GAME

The Internet is your source for a free and fun game about the business of reporting news. You'll find the directions at http://kootweb.com/games/newsgame.html. Find two or more friends to play with you.

CHECK IT OUT

Association for Education in Journalism and Mass Communication
University of South Carolina
1621 College Street
Columbia, South Carolina 29208-0251

Community College Journalism Association
San Antonio College
1300 San Pedro Avenue
San Antonio, Texas 78212-4299

Down Jones Newspapers Fund, Inc.
P.O. Box 300
Princeton, New Jersey 08543-0300

National Newspaper Association
1627 K Street NW, Suite 400
Washington, D.C. 20006

Newspaper Association of America Foundation
11600 Sunrise Valley Drive
Reston, Virginia 22091-1412

Newspaper Center
Box 17407
Dulles International Airport
Washington, D.C. 20041

Radio and Television News Directors Foundation
1000 Connecticut Avenue NW, Suite 615
Washington, D.C. 20036

Society of Broadcast Engineers, Inc.
8445 Keystone Crossing, Suite 140
Indianapolis, Indiana 46240-2454

GET ACQUAINTED

Mark Miller, News Reporter

CAREER PATH

CHILDHOOD ASPIRATION: To be an attorney or clergyman.

FIRST JOB: As a teenager, he peeled 200 pounds of onions a night in a sandwich shop.

CURRENT JOB: News director for WBAL in Baltimore, Maryland.

TOTALLY RESPONSIBLE

Although he started with the station as a news reporter, Mark Miller is now responsible for the entire news staff of the radio station. That means he oversees the reporting of the daily news of the nation, the city, and the world; it also includes weather, traffic, business, politics, and special events. He manages an annual budget of over $1 million!

Each day he holds "story meetings." He and his staff discuss what's going on that day, assign new stories, and map out the broadcast as best they can. Each reporter does what it takes to get the story together, writes it up, coordinates details such as special pre-taped interviews, and assumes responsibility for getting the story ready for broadcast.

THE EDWARD R. MURROW AWARD

In the broadcasting industry the most prestigious news award is the Edward R. Murrow Award. It's like getting an Oscar. Miller's station won six in the last four years for overall excellence in reporting and specifically for sports and feature reporting.

A few years ago the station won the award for an investigative report they did about the city comptroller. They did their homework and snooped around a bit, and they found out that money was being paid out to places it shouldn't have been. They uncovered the story and put an end to the waste and wrong-doing.

AN ENDURANCE TEST

Miller says one of the most important qualities of being a news reporter is having endurance. In 1987, in order to cover a train wreck nearby (the worst accident in the history of Amtrak), he worked nonstop from the Sunday afternoon when it happened until the following Tuesday morning. He was on the air almost the whole time. That's a long time to stay focused and prepared (not to mention awake and alert).

A PIECE OF HISTORY

He's also been part of history in the making. When Pope John Paul II came to Baltimore on a visit, he served as the radio pool coordinator. That meant that he provided the news to networks all over the world. It was a unique historical event, probably the only time in Miller's lifetime that the pope will come to his city. He was there, watched it happen, and got a unique behind-the-scenes look at the entire event.

THANK YOU!

His junior high and high school English teachers played a big part in preparing Miller for what he is doing now. They encouraged him to excel in literature. They helped him hone his writing skills and put him on the path to seeking out news.

MILLER'S RECIPE FOR A GOOD REPORTER

Good reporters have to have perseverance, patience, and dedication. The job is fast-paced, demanding, and quite frankly, lots of hard work. Only a few people have the talent to be a good reporter. Fewer still are willing to work as hard as it takes to succeed. But the rewards are great.

Politician

SKILL SET

✔ HISTORY
✔ TALKING
✔ WRITING

SHORTCUTS

GO talk to your state senator or representative.

READ anything you can by or about Thomas Jefferson, Abraham Lincoln, or Eleanor Roosevelt.

TRY running for student council in your school.

WHAT IS A POLITICIAN?

Politicians are the people who have been chosen through an election process to govern a very specific geographical area—be it a small town, a state, or an entire nation. Most politicians are affiliated with a political party. The United States is currently a two-party system of Democrats and Republicans. Each party is based on mutual agreement on a platform of important issues. Each party chooses candidates for each election and backs them with time, finances, and other forms of support to help them win.

In a system based on the premise of government by the people, of the people, and for the people, there are a few hard and fast rules about who can run for an elected position. The basics include some age restrictions (for example, you must be at least 35 to run for president), U.S. citizenship, and other residency requirements. More often than not, those who are elected to political office are fairly well educated; however, a politician's educational background can run anywhere from political science and law to agronomy and education.

Probably, the single most important trait for a politician is to have the so-called fire in the belly, that is, the drive and sense of purpose necessary to pursue political goals in spite of very challenging circumstances. A tradition of commitment and service to one's community and political party can also make a difference on election day.

Behind every politician—the winners and the losers—is a staff of political professionals, who are both paid and unpaid. There are any number of clerks, campaign managers, press officers, media managers, research assistants, bill writers, speech writers, pages, and runners. These types of jobs provide an avenue for others with a desire to be involved in the political process without actually running for office themselves. Working as a "public servant" at any number of government agencies—on the local, state, or federal levels—is another means to serve one's country and make a difference in important issues.

TRY IT OUT

RUN, RUN, RUN

Get involved in your own school politics. Run for student council (or form one if your school doesn't have one). If you aren't ready or interested in running yourself, volunteer to serve as campaign manager for another worthy candidate.

Make an official plan detailing how you hope to get yourself or your candidate elected. Include ideas for posters, outlines for speeches, and other materials that will help get your ideas across to your voters.

CAMPAIGN CITY

Volunteer to work on a political campaign in your area, whether for a mayoral candidate or a school board candidate. If someone in your town is running for a state or federal position, such as senator, volunteer to help with that campaign.

There is always plenty of work to be done—everything from stuffing envelopes to putting out posters. Make it a point to spend time with the experienced campaigners and watch what they do to run a campaign. Keep samples of all the campaign materials (for your candidate and the opponent) and note which tactics are most effective.

Look in the phone book for the Democratic or Republican headquarters in your town. Call them and see how you can help.

A LAW IS BORN

After all the speeches are made and the votes are counted, a politician's job has just begun. The following ideas will help you find out what a politician does during a typical day.

- Sit in on a school board meeting or town council meeting. Note the pros and cons of each issue being discussed.
- Take a tour of your state capitol during the legislative session. Sit in the visitors' gallery and listen to issues being debated in the Senate and House.
- Make an appointment to visit with your state or national senator or representative.
- Follow an issue by keeping track of its coverage in the local newspaper. Clip every article you can find about the process and keep notes on the details.
- Find an issue that you really believe in and become an advocate on its behalf. Writing letters, getting signatures on petitions, organizing activities to gain public attention, and speaking out in appropriate ways are all part of the process of getting good laws passed and bad laws repealed.

GET UP CLOSE AND PERSONAL

Take time to volunteer in any community activity. You'll get to meet people and see some of your town's issues firsthand. Try volunteering at a child-care center or a senior citizen's center, tutor younger children, or help clean up a park or roadside.

There are many ways to make a difference in your community. For some great ideas take a look at *150 Ways Teens Can Make a Difference* by Marian Salzman and Teresa Reisgies (New York: Peterson's Guides, 1991).

GET A HAMMER AND SOME NAILS

Join in the effort to help the homeless. Habitat for Humanity provides an opportunity to work closely with people while building housing for low-income families. Check your newspaper for information about local projects or contact the international headquarters: Habitat for Humanity International, 121 Habitat Street, Americus, Georgia 31709. It's a great way to spend a summer or spring break.

ON-LINE POLITICS

For information on each of the political parties, go on-line to their respective websites. The Democratic Party camps out at http://www.democrats.org/party. The Republicans can be found at http://www.rnc.org. Additional information on government and the political process can be found through the League of Women Voters at http://www.lwv.org.

CHECK IT OUT

American Political Science Association
1527 New Hampshire Avenue NW
Washington, D.C. 20036

Democratic National Committee
430 South Capitol Street SE
Washington, D.C. 20003

International City/County Management Association
777 North Capitol Street NE, Suite 500
Washington, D.C. 20002

League of Women Voters of the United States
1730 M Street NW
Washington, D.C. 20036-4505

National Conference of State Legislatures
1560 Broadway
Denver, Colorado 80202

Republican National Committee
301 First Street SE
Washington, D.C. 20003

GET ACQUAINTED

Gail S. Schoettler, Colorado State Lieutenant Governor

CAREER PATH

CHILDHOOD ASPIRATION: To learn all she could about everything.

FIRST JOB: Working cattle on her family's ranch.

CURRENT JOB: Lieutenant governor of the state of Colorado.

SPEECH, SPEECH!

There isn't a typical day for this busy politician, but Gail Schoettler will usually give two to four speeches every day! If you want to be a politician, you must be prepared to speak in front of groups of people—with and without advance preparation.

Schoettler is obviously comfortable doing this. Each of her speeches sounds as though she is talking personally with each listener. Even on the telephone (where she spends another chunk of time each day), she is fully focused on her listener and the issues being discussed at that moment.

BUILDING BRIDGES

Schoettler deals with many different kinds of people on many different issues and problems. She was a cochair for the Summit of the Eight conference held in Denver. (The Summit of Eight was an important meeting that brought the heads of eight nations together to discuss international issues.) This meant she had to be sure things ran smoothly, and she had to greet the president of the United States, his counterparts from seven other countries, as well as all kinds of diplomats, press people, and other VIPs. She also had to be aware of the cultural values each person brought to the summit and the issues they found most important. Building bridges between the people and their opinions about the issues was the toughest part of the process for Schoettler. Reaching a point where everyone agrees on a solution takes a lot of hard work, but the end result makes it well worth the effort.

CHILDREN'S MUSEUM

At one point in her career, Schoettler helped to start a museum just for children. Her bridge-building skills came in handy for this project too, especially in getting everyone to agree about how to make the museum financially self-sufficient. She worked with many volunteers who could spend a little time on the project. There was one crisis after another as the project began to take shape. As she brought people closer together, these problems were solved collectively, using everyone's best ideas. That was 24 years ago. The Children's Museum is still operating today, and it brings joy and education to thousands of Colorado children each year.

BE TRUE TO YOURSELF

The most important value to Schoettler is honesty. A politician often has to make unpopular decisions. At times like that, Schoettler says that it's important to be true to your own principles and values. Even if the decision isn't popular or if someone disagrees, you need to stand by your decision and do what you think is right.

POLITICAL ROLE MODELS

No politician gets to the top without someone to help and guide them. Schoettler has found this guidance in many places. The governor has helped her with advice and direction. She also admires John F. Kennedy for his ability to inspire an entire generation and Eleanor Roosevelt for her political instincts and her role as first lady of the United States. She suggests that you find out all you can about Eleanor Roosevelt and how her work influenced an earlier generation of Americans.

A VISION TO SERVE

Whether it's a town, a state, or a country that you are governing, there are always many problems waiting to be solved. While the governor will often ask Schoettler to take action on a particular problem, the lieutenant governor also picks other issues that need her attention by talking (and listening!) to her voters. Public school education, international trade, and family are very important to her. These are the areas she likes to focus on. She has spent much of her time helping Colorado's young people realize that a good education gives them many different career choices.

Schoettler has a vision for her state that includes a good education for young people, good family life, a beautiful environment, and healthy international trade. She communicates that vision through her speeches. She works every day to bring that vision into reality by building bridges among many different people.

Publicist

SKILL SET

- ✔ ART
- ✔ TALKING
- ✔ WRITING

SHORTCUTS

GO to a major event in your town (a concert, sporting event, or movie premiere), and look at all promotional materials—news ads, feature stories, posters, and other promotions.

READ the lifestyles feature section of a major newspaper. Many of the articles you'll find there are the result of a publicists' efforts in promoting a client or a product.

TRY helping to promote the next school dance or sporting event.

WHAT IS A PUBLICIST?

Movie stars have them, major sports figures have them, politicians rely on them, and so does virtually every major corporation, government agency, nonprofit organization, and school. Publicists, also called public relations specialists (PR specialist, for short), help build a positive public image for all of these entities. They do this by generating publicity for their clients.

In an ideal situation, the publicity revolves around something good that has happened. For instance, a publicist might help a movie star promote a new movie or a corporation launch a new product. But publicists also have to be ready to respond to negative publicity about their client as well. This might involve some sort of tragedy or a big blunder on the part of their client. They have to be prepared, often at a moment's notice, to put a positive "spin" on even the worst of circumstances.

One of the earliest and still most famous business promoters was P. T. Barnum (of Barnum & Bailey Circus fame). He once said, "There is no such thing as bad publicity." A good publicist makes this statement true for his or her clients.

In order to promote their clients, publicists develop public relations campaigns that involve tasks such as writing press releases, organizing media conferences, designing brochures and other promotional publications, and booking clients on

radio and television talk shows. Three important details can determine the success of a public relations campaign.

First is the newsworthiness of the information being presented. If a press release, for example, is simply a blatant advertisement for the client, it may not work. The PR specialist must develop angles or hooks that meet the needs of each media source's audience. This makes for a winning situation for both sides. The PR specialist gets the exposure, and the media source scores points for sharing interesting information with their readers.

The second aspect of a successful PR campaign is that the publicist has done the homework required and has produced top-notch materials. The media receives mountains of press packets every day. It takes some ingenuity to get one seen, let alone read, by a harried reporter.

The third key to a successful PR campaign is developing positive, personal relationships with media representatives. Such a relationship is achieved over time by producing consistent quality work and building a trustworthy reputation. Once that point is reached, reporters know to consider information that a specific publicist sends.

Sometimes people get public relations mixed up with marketing or advertising. Although the goals of both efforts are often similar, the methods are completely different. For one thing, publicity is free. Advertising costs big bucks.

There is a catch, of course. With publicity there is no guarantee that the media will "bite" and carry the story, and even if they do, there is no telling how they'll present the pitch. With advertising, you get exactly what you pay for and have complete control over how the message is conveyed.

To become a publicist requires a college degree with a major in public relations, journalism, advertising, or communications. To actually break into the field, experience in television, radio, or print journalism is often required. Some corporations will also want a publicist to have knowledge of the company's industry as well, although this can often be learned on the job.

Potential publicists should take advantage of every opportunity to get their name and work in print. A well-rounded, professional portfolio full of published articles, multimedia presentations, and other publications can open important career-enhancing doors.

P. T. Barnum summed up the role of publicists nicely when he said, "Without publicity a terrible thing happens—NOTHING."

TRY IT OUT

WHAT'S IN IT FOR ME?

Publicists are continually reminded that unless the audience has an interest in what they have to say, there will be no audience. Consumers want to know, "What's in it for me?"

Look at any good advertisement (key word here is good) to see this principle at work. Go through a magazine or newspaper and cut out three or four advertisements. See if you can identify the key benefits aimed at interesting you, the audience. For instance, does it mention things such as saving you money or improving your life? Mind you, just because the ad seems to promise miraculous results, doesn't mean that it's true. Beware of hype!

SPIN A TALE

This is a two-part project. First, take a trip to the library. Find out all you can about Benedict Arnold (he was a U.S. general who was considered a traitor during the Revolutionary War). Then, pretend that you are his PR person. What kind of "spin" could you put on his alleged betrayal that would get him off the hook?

Prepare a press kit containing your response. Make sure to include information about his background and a press release containing all the who, what, where, when, how, and why details that you can to try to save his neck.

IF YOU CAN PULL THIS OFF . . .

Write a compelling press release explaining why you think it would be a good thing to add an extra half hour to every school day. Remember that your appeal must include benefits for your audience, which would consist of students, teachers, and parents.

To test the effectiveness of your pitch, attach a petition to be signed by those who agree with your idea. See how many friends, teachers, and parents you can convince to sign on the dotted line. If you can pull this one off, you definitely show promise for becoming a great publicist!

SPIN A SPILL

It's been a while since it happened (March 24, 1989, to be precise), but the oil spill by the Exxon *Valdez* oil tanker that ran aground remains one of the classic public relations nightmares. Find out all you can about how the company handled this situation.

You might start with the Internet. Two websites to look at are the following:

- http://www.api.org/resources/valdez/
- http://www.alaska.net/~ospic/rpln.html

You can also request information from ARLIS, 3150 C Street, Suite 100, Anchorage, Alaska 99503 (or call them at 800-283-7745).

Make a list of the mistakes they made and the positive points they scored. Tally them up and decide how well the Exxon PR department handled this disaster.

SPIN PATROL

Nobody does PR like show business. Hollywood typically invests major money in promoting each new movie and television show. The Internet is your source for Hollywood's spins on the latest releases. Find out who does it best at http://www.hollywood.com.

BLUE JEANS AND CAREERS

Levi's Jeans for Women provides an excellent example of mixing business with pleasure at their website: http://syiner.women.com/work/go/publicist. With a subtle ulterior motive of selling more jeans, the site provides valuable information about a variety of interesting career options for women, including publicist.

Take a reality check while you're there: How do you feel about getting up at 4:00 A.M. to ensure the success of your client's product launch or appearance on *Good Morning America?*

CHECK IT OUT

American Marketing Association
250 South Wacker Drive
Chicago, Illinois 60606

American Society for
Health Care Marketing and
Public Relations
American Hospital Association
One North Franklin Street
Chicago, Illinois 60606

Council of Sales Promotion
Agencies
750 Summer Street
Stamford, Connecticut 06901

Promotion Marketing Association
of America, Inc.
322 Eighth Avenue, Suite 1201
New York, New York 10001

PR Reporter
P.O. Box 600
Exeter, New Hampshire 03833

Public Relations Society of
America, Inc.
33 Irving Place
New York, New York 10003-2376

GET ACQUAINTED

John Kehl, Publicist

CAREER PATH

CHILDHOOD ASPIRATION: To be an entrepreneur, owning a business that let him do something creative.

FIRST JOB: Cutting grass in his neighborhood.

CURRENT JOB: Associate director of sports information for the National Association of Intercollegiate Athletics.

JUST THE STATS

John Kehl spends much of his time preparing information about many different sports teams for the national media. His work deals with 23 different sports played at more than 350 different U.S. colleges. This means pulling together lots of statistics, adding up numbers, and keeping track of how each team is doing.

FROM HOME RUNS TO HEAVEN

Working with so many different teams has been Kehl's stairway to heaven. He says, "For most of the players getting a good education is really important. But, it's great to see how they enhance and balance their classroom learning with sports and a competitive spirit."

Kehl got here via Switzerland. He was working previously for the International Rowing Federation when one day, he got a phone call from someone who he'd met earlier from the Colorado Rockies organization. The caller asked if he'd be interested in an interview with the team's management. Would he be interested? You bet!

After the interview he was offered an internship in the public relations department. Like many successful internships, this one turned into a full-time, paid position as a public relations assistant. There he got a lot of the experience he needed to be prepared for his current job.

MAKE IT SHINE

PR is all about giving things value—making them shine. Kehl says he isn't a marketer, just someone who presents information honestly in the best light possible. His job is to give someone a positive feeling about the sport. The hot thing about what he does is being able to talk to so many different schools about so many different sports. Sharing that excitement with national media is just part of what makes this a great job.

A WAY OF LIFE

Kehl eats, sleeps, walks, and talks sports. That includes golf, volleyball, baseball, football, tennis, track, soccer, softball, wrestling, swimming and diving, and cross country. Keeping track of both men's and women's teams for each of these sports, their rankings, the national ratings, and all the stats on the players, as well as getting the info out, is a big job, but Kehl loves it. Whether he's at home or on the road he really gets a kick out of sports.

A typical day begins at 7:00 or 8:00 A.M. and doesn't end until well into the night if he's at a championship event. It's hard work, but lots of fun especially since it's amateur sports. Kehl says most of the kids are in it for the love of the game. That makes it a great place to be.

A WINNING COMBINATION

If you want to work in public relations, Kehl advises that you make sure you learn how to write. Learn how to get your point across quickly and clearly. Intern as much as possible. You never know when a contact you make will turn into a long-term, exciting job.

P.S.

If you are particularly interested in sports PR, get involved in your athletic department's events. Keep the stats. Keep a scorebook.

Retailer

SKILL SET

✔ BUSINESS

✔ COMPUTERS

✔ TALKING

SHORTCUTS

GO to a shopping mall nearby and notice all the different kinds of shops.

READ *Ben and Jerry's Double Dip* by Ben Cohen and Jerry Greenfield (New York: Simon and Schuster, 1997).

TRY working in your school or neighborhood store.

WHAT IS A RETAILER?

People everywhere make a regular habit of buying things. Food, clothes, books, furniture, tools—you name it and someone wants to buy it. Retailers are the people who work in the stores that sell products for public consumption.

Retail stores come in all shapes and sizes. Some are independently owned and operated by someone as a private business. Sometimes called "mom and pop" businesses, these stores usually specialize in a particular type of merchandise, such as sports equipment or flowers. Other stores are franchises or branches of a major corporation. There are many fast-food chains that fall into this category. Another kind of retailer is a big department store. Then there are the more upscale shopping mall stores that specialize primarily in clothing and accessories as well as the superstores that carry a little bit of almost everything.

Big or little, all retail stores rely on a competent sales staff and effective managers to succeed. The sales staff might include cashiers, courtesy clerks, stockroom workers, and sales floor assistants. Most of these positions are entry level and many are available as part-time jobs for high school and college students.

Working in a retail store is one way to get the experience needed to become a retail manager. Retail managers and store owners often wear more than one hat around the store. They supervise and schedule the sales staff and are responsible for inventory control, customer service complaints, and training programs. They are responsible for the overall success of the store.

In larger stores and chains, there are several levels of management with the department manager being the first rung on the career ladder. In a big store, the store manager is in charge of the department managers and sets the policies and programs that guide the store. Higher up the ladder may be district, area, or regional managers who are responsible for more than one store.

As one might expect, the higher up the ladder you go, the more training you'll need. Most managers begin their careers working as part of the retail sales staff. In some cases, the store itself provides comprehensive training that might last from one week to a year or more. Other stores hire only management with a college-level degree in a business-related area such as business administration or marketing.

Two other professions associated with the retail industry are manufacturer's representatives (or reps) and buyers. The manufacturer's rep actually represents a specific manufacturer and the products it produces. Be it sports shoes or perfume, these people typically work in a specific "territory" and travel around to service established accounts and set up new ones. The person they are most likely to deal with at a larger store is the buyer.

Buyers are responsible for choosing the merchandise that is sold in the store. This requires an accurate sense of what the store's customers will want to buy.

No matter what your ultimate ambition, if you are interested in a retailing career, a good place to start is with a high school cooperative education program. These programs provide an opportunity to earn while you gain firsthand experience in the business.

Overall, competition for customers in the retail industry can be as fierce as it is thrilling. There is always another way a customer can spend that dollar. A retailer's main mission is to find customers and keep them coming back for more.

TRY IT OUT

CLEAN OUT THE GARAGE!

Ask your family what they think about getting rid of some of the excess clutter around your house. If they sound interested, team up with them to host a garage sale (also known as a yard sale, tag sale, etc.). Clean out your attic, your garage, your basement, and your bedroom.

Organize and price everything that you decide to sell. Arrange things on tables, racks, or in boxes. Make it as easy as possible to spot all the bargains. Make signs to advertise the event and consider placing a classified ad in the local paper. The better you get the word out, the more potential buyers you'll attract.

On the day of the event, be prepared with about $20 in change, a designated spot to keep the cash, and a notebook to keep track of each sale.

At the end of the day, tally up the sales and invite the whole family out for dinner to celebrate.

COMPARISON SHOPPER

Visit two or more stores that specialize in the same kinds of merchandise. Grocery stores, hardware stores, and discount department stores are some ideas to consider. Walk through the store and note how the departments and merchandise are displayed. List the three things you like best and the three things you like least about each store. While you are there, jot down the prices of several items. Find the same items in each store and compare the prices.

BE A SECRET SHOPPER

Call your local chamber of commerce and ask if it has a secret shopper program. Secret shoppers are people who go into a store, buy something, see what kind of service they get, and file a report on the results. Volunteer to do some secret shopping around town (sometimes the chambers will pay you to do this). You'll need good observation and reporting skills to get this job done.

DO THE MALL CRAWL

Take a walk through your local shopping mall. Make a list of all the different specialty stores. Visit as many as you can and note what methods they are using to get people to come into their store. Maybe they use a sale, a special promotion, or eye-catching displays. Hang around for a while and count how many customers actually enter each store to gauge how well each method works.

SELL, SELL, SELL

If you are a student currently enrolled in any school in the world, you probably won't lack for opportunities to get some good sales experience. Every PTA, sports team, and band is constantly looking for ways to raise money. Get involved in these fund-raisers and help find creative ways to support these worthy causes.

CHECK IT OUT

American Management Association
135 West 50th Street
New York, New York 10020

Food Marketing Institute
800 Connecticut Avenue NW
Washington, D.C. 20006-2701

National Association of Convenience Stores
1605 King Street
Alexandria, Virginia 22314

National Automobile Dealers Association
8400 Westpark Drive
McLean, Virginia 22102-3591

National Retail Federation
701 Pennsylvania Avenue NW, Suite 710
Washington, D.C. 20004

Service Station Dealers of America
9420 Annapolis Road, Suite 307
Lanham, Maryland 20706

GET ACQUAINTED

Debby Harris, Retailer

CAREER PATH

CHILDHOOD ASPIRATION: To be a dietician.

FIRST JOB: Baby-sat for neighbor with five kids. She did lots of cooking and ironing.

CURRENT JOB: Owner of a specialty retail business called the Made in Colorado Shoppe.

HATS FOR EVERY DAY

Debby Harris compares her job to wearing lots of different hats. She gets to work early in the morning to work on the computer, set up the store for the day, sweep the sidewalk, and water the flowers. Once the store is open for business, she waits on customers, keeps the store tidy, and restocks the shelves. In between customers, she tries to sneak a minute here and there to order more stock or unpack boxes of new merchandise. When the store closes, she sits down to total the day's receipts, pay bills, and do other accounting chores. In short, she does it all.

THREE CHEERS FOR THE CUSTOMER

Harris knows that her customers are the most important part of her store. She greets customers as they walk in the door and tries to talk to each one. By the end of the day, she sometimes feels as though her smile is pasted on. But it's meeting all the interesting people that keeps the job fun. Harris especially enjoys helping each person find just what he or she is looking for.

BIG STORE BACKGROUND

Harris got her start working for Nordstrom's, a very large department store with a reputation for providing excellent customer service. When her husband asked her to help out for a little while in his small-town pharmacy, she started selling fudge in one corner of the store. It was just the thing to bring splurging tourists into the store.

It wasn't long before her fudge corner grew. Now Harris owns her own boutique selling specialty gift items. Everything she sells is made in her home state of Colorado. This special feature attracts curious tourists and gives her the chance to brag a bit about one of her favorite places in the world—her state.

SCARY START

Made in Colorado Shoppe is Harris' store—for better or worse. She's completely responsible for everything! That can be a scary thought, but for Harris it's been a great motivator.

Before she opened the doors, she became an expert in the business. She learned all she could about store layout, product displays, lighting, inventory, and financing a small business. This process involved a ton of research. She talked to hundreds of people who had opened similar businesses in other towns. She interviewed potential customers to find out what they wanted (she still does this regularly) and how much they wanted to pay for things. Fortunately, she had help from an experienced associate who helped her learn the ropes. This mentor was a lifesaver and taught her never to be afraid to ask for help.

While her other retail experience has served her well, she found it was a whole new ball game being on her own. She was solely responsible for the success or failure of the store. It was scary at first. But, it's made her eventual success all the more sweeter.

SECRETS OF HER SUCCESS

Harris credits her continuing success as a retailer to three basic principles and shares them with anyone looking into the field:

- Watch trends. Things change constantly. Be ready to go with the flow.
- Perception is everything. Take an ordinary item, make it look interesting on the shelf, and you'll drastically increase your chances of selling it.
- The customer is king.

She also teaches her employees to ring the register: Once they learn how to provide good customer service, the sales follow naturally.

Social Worker

SKILL SET

- ✔ COMPUTERS
- ✔ HISTORY
- ✔ TALKING

SHORTCUTS

GO get involved in your local D.A.R.E. (Drug Abuse Resistance Education) program. Contact your school counselor or local police department for details.

READ all about Jane Addams (the author of nine books on social work) and her work with women and children in Chicago in 1889, when she cofounded Hull House.

TRY solving your community's problems. Check out some of the problems headlined in the local newspaper. List your ideas for solving them.

WHAT IS A SOCIAL WORKER?

Social workers and counselors listen to people, ask questions, and find useful resources to help people solve all kinds of problems. There's certainly no shortage of problems to deal with in this profession. Drug and alcohol addictions, child abuse, homelessness, and people with disabilities are just a few of the challenges social worker have to face every day.

Some social workers specialize in helping people with emotional or mental problems. Others deal exclusively with children. Quite often this type of work involves helping someone who doesn't have anywhere else to turn. For instance, some social workers help people who are seriously ill with diseases such as AIDS find someone to take care of them or connect them with a hospice. Counselors also specialize in dealing with certain types of problems such as injury rehabilitation, terminal illness, grief, marriage and family, and problem pregnancies.

One likely place to find a social worker is in a school just like yours. Here social workers help students deal with problems such as cutting classes, flunking out of school, or taking drugs. Other school counselors help students find just the right college for them.

Increasingly in demand are gerontological social workers. These social workers assist the elderly with things like finding transportation to doctor's appointments, nursing home care, and other services.

Yet another type of counseling involves helping people find or change their careers. You might even want to talk to one of these counselors in your search!

To become a social worker you must be licensed by the state in which you work and complete some very specific education. A bachelor's degree is a must and a minimum! If you want to work in any of the health-care fields, you will also need a master's degree. A doctorate is required if you want to teach social work at a college or university.

With so many problems in the world today, you can really take your pick of the area in which you want to work. Social work is all about helping people and families get along better. The work can be heartwarming, but sometimes it's heartbreaking. It takes a caring, strong person who's not afraid to deal with the best and worst life has to offer to succeed as a social worker.

TRY IT OUT

GO SURFING

Check out the National Association of Social Workers' home page at http://www.naswdc.org. While you are there, take a look at the National Association of Social Workers Code of Ethics. These are the standards of behavior that govern good social work. Think you can measure up?

GO SNOOPING

Check out a copy of Margaret Gibelman's book *What Social Workers Do* (Washington, D.C.: National Association of Social Workers, 1995). Make a list of all the ideas and specialties mentioned in the book. Put a star by those that interest you most and find out about agencies and programs in your area that serve those kinds of needs.

Here are a few jobs you're bound to learn about.

admissions counselor
cultural resource manager
detention officer
drug counselor
family counselor
probation officer
social work coordinator
substance abuse counselor
youth care worker

What other ones can you find?

JUST DO IT!

Now's the time to find out if a career in social work is right for you. Fortunately, there are plenty of opportunities to test your helping skills. Volunteer anywhere that you'll have a chance to meet people. This can include nursing homes, child-care centers, or food-delivery programs. Many elder-care homes have a need for people to just read and talk to the residents.

The benefits of volunteering are twofold. You can make a difference while you find out how you like working with people with problems.

If you need ideas about kinds of volunteer jobs, check out the following books:

McMillon, Bill. *Volunteer Vacations*. Chicago: Chicago Review Press, 1997.

Salzman, Marian, and Teresa Reisgies. *150 Ways Teens Can Make a Difference*. New York: Peterson's Guides, 1991.

WHAT IF. . .

What if one of your friends was in trouble? How would you help them? Using your phone book, make a list of all the resources available to solve their problem. Call or visit each place on your list and see if you can find five more resources.

Jot down a few notes about what each resources does (include phone numbers and addresses). Organize your sources on notecards and keep them in a file box. As you become aware of new resources, add an information card to your file.

PLAY DEAR ABBY

Every newspaper has at least one advice column. People write letters explaining their problem and the "expert" advice columnist gives them ideas on how to solve it.

Try your hand at the advice business with the help of your local newspaper and a roll of adhesive tape. First, find and cut out the advice column in the newspaper, but don't read it yet. Next, ask a friend or family member to tape bits of paper over all the advice columnist's answers so all you can see are the questions.

Now, read each question carefully and write an appropriate response. This part may involve some detective work! You may have to find out a little more about the problem before offering adequate advice. What resources are there that can help? This is where the Yellow Pages and the local library can come in handy.

Finally, take a look at the advice columnist's responses and see how your answers compare. (If you really get the hang of things, you might consider approaching your school newspaper with an offer to write an advice column for them.)

CHECK IT OUT

American Counseling Association
5999 Stevenson Avenue
Alexandria, Virginia 22304
800-347-6647

Council for Accreditation of Counseling and Related Educational Programs
5999 Stevenson Avenue
Alexandria, Virginia 22304

Council on Social Work Education
P.O. Box 2072
Alexandria, Virginia 22314-3412

National Association of Social Workers
IC-Career Information
750 First Street NE, Suite 700
Washington, D.C. 20002-4241

National Association of Workforce Development Professionals
1620 I Street NW, Suite 30
Washington, D.C. 20006

National Network for Social Work Managers, Inc.
1316 New Hampshire Avenue NW, Suite 602
Washington, D.C. 20036

School Social Work Association of America
P.O. Box 2072
Northlake, Illinois 80164

GET ACQUAINTED

Bob Davis, Career Counselor

CAREER PATH

CHILDHOOD ASPIRATION: People have been the focus of his career plans since he was in the eighth grade: He first thought about teaching but then discovered social work.

FIRST JOB: As a Boy Scout, he bartered for a hatchet by working as a parking lot attendant.

CURRENT JOB: Self-employment director for the Private Industry Council in Wisconsin.

CHOICES, CHOICES, AND MORE CHOICES

One of the best parts of Bob Davis' job is the fact that he gets to work with lots of different kinds of people. During his career he has gone from working with children to working with prisoners to working with men in an abuse prevention program. He currently specializes in helping older workers.

One of the most exciting projects he's ever worked on was helping the state of Wisconsin move developmentally disabled children into less restrictive environments. This involved only seven social workers in the state, hours of talking to people, and lots of detective work!

MAKE THE CONNECTION

Now Davis focuses on bringing possible employers and workers together. He looks for ways to make a connection between needs: a need for work and a need for a worker. This can involve some complex coordinating, because he has to find just the right worker for the job and he has to find just the right job for the worker.

He also teaches classes to older workers who want to start their own businesses. He developed his own approach to entrepreneurship and enjoys watching people's businesses take off and succeed.

TWO SIDES OF THE STORY

To accomplish his work, Davis must interview both the employees and the employers, so he gets to hear both sides of the story. Careful listening and posing the right questions are key to making a successful match.

In his role as a social worker, people often tell him things that no one else knows. Davis must keep this sensitive information secret, unless keeping it a secret poses a danger to the person or others. This is called confidentiality, and it is one of the most important skills a social worker must possess.

While it sometimes seems that the role of the social worker is to solve problems, Davis says that his job really depends on asking the right questions so that people find the solution themselves.

MENTORS MADE THE DIFFERENCE

Davis worked with a sergeant major while they were both in the army. This sergeant major had put himself through college (after serving in the military) and then got drafted during two wars. He finally made the army his career and spent his time there helping soldiers and the people around him. Davis says the encouragement and example of this sergeant major helped him get started on the right foot.

WHAT'S THE WORST THING ABOUT HIS JOB?

Writer's cramp. There's lots of paperwork in this job. Davis spends about 40 percent of his time filling out forms and reports for the government. So, work on your computer skills.

Speech Pathologist

SKILL SET

- ✔ ADVENTURE
- ✔ TALKING
- ✔ SCIENCE

SHORTCUTS

GO volunteer to tutor someone in an English as a Second Language (ESL) program.

READ *My Fair Lady*, a play written by Alan J. Lerner and Frederick Loewe (or watch the movie version on video).

TRY repeating the following phrase three times in a row without tripping over your tongue—"Peter Piper picked a peck of pickled peppers."

WHAT IS A SPEECH PATHOLOGIST?

Imagine life without the ability to speak or be understood. It changes even the most basic tasks in major ways. Since spoken words are the foundation for a person's ability to communicate, not being able to speak would alter a person's life in a huge way.

Speech pathologists work with people of all ages to help them use their voices to communicate clearly and effectively. This might involve working with a child born with a birth defect such as a cleft lip or one with developmental disabilities that result in having trouble producing sounds or being understood. It could involve helping someone who has damaged their vocal cords due to excessive use or has developed a voice disorder. Some speech pathologists work with patients who are recovering from illnesses such as strokes or head injuries to help them relearn vital communication skills. Others work with professionals who are trying to improve their diction and presentation skills or rid themselves of an obvious accent.

The work of speech pathologists usually consists of a three-step process. First, they must assess the nature of the problem. Speech pathologists use a variety of tests and special instruments to help them diagnose speech problems.

The second step involves therapy or treatment of the problem. This can be done on a one-on-one basis or with a small group. Speech pathologists draw from a wide array of activities and treatment plans to help correct various speech problems.

The final step is evaluation. In the best of circumstances, this step is used to determine when someone is completely rehabilitated and free of speech disorders. Other times it is used to gauge the effectiveness of the treatment plan and make necessary adjustments.

Audiologists could be considered "career cousins" to speech pathologists. What speech pathologists are to speech, audiologists are to hearing. They provide similar types of care to people with different needs. Sometimes their work intersects with one another, and they must team up to provide effective care. Put simply, audiology and speech pathology are about helping people hear and be heard.

Schools, clinics, hospitals, rehabilitation centers, and research centers are typical places where both audiologists and speech pathologists might work. Both jobs reflect a unique blend of both the education and healthcare fields.

In order to meet certification requirements of the American Speech, Language, and Hearing Associations, practicing speech pathologists must earn a master's degree in speech-language pathology or audiology. While a master's is considered the standard credential in this field, some states allow people with a bachelor's degree to work under special supervision with students in schools.

TRY IT OUT

ACT THE PART

Drama can be an enjoyable way to enhance your speaking skills because you have to slip into someone else's voice and mannerisms in order to act different parts. Make a point of auditioning for the next school play. While you are learning your lines, make a conscious effort to improve your enunciation, diction, and projection skills. Your drama coach will be more than happy to help you achieve these goals.

WALK IN THEIR SHOES

Sometimes when something comes easily for you, it is hard to understand why it's so difficult for someone else. In order to be effective, speech pathologists must be able to understand the frustration that their clients feel at not being able to communicate.

For a quick lesson in empathy, check out some foreign language tapes from the library or video store. Listen to a short dialogue segment several times until you think you can repeat what is being said. Keep trying until you get it right.

The focus, the failure, the frustration you may feel at trying to make these foreign sounds are precisely what some people feel just trying to say hello in their own language.

EXPLORE SHAKESPEARE

Some say that William Shakespeare was the greatest writer of plays who ever lived. He wrote his plays many, *many* years ago. In fact, he wrote them so long ago that the language was quite different than the English we use today.

Take a trip to the library and check out a book of his plays. *Romeo and Juliet*, *Much Ado About Nothing*, and *The Taming of the Shrew* are all interesting plays to read. Now pick a part and memorize some of the lines of that part. Speak clearly. Have someone else read the other parts for you and see if you can speak your lines so that your friends all understand you easily.

TALK TO THE ANIMALS

Have you ever wondered how dogs and cats communicate? They make sounds, but they don't use words like we do. Carefully observe the animals in your life. If you don't have pets of your own, visit an animal shelter or pet shop or just sit on a park bench and listen to the birds.

Listen to the sounds they make. See if you can figure out what the different sounds mean. Some pitches may signal danger, and others may signal hunger, while others may be friendly chitchat. See if you can imitate some of the sounds they make.

VISIT A GROWLING OLD GEEZER

A growling old geezer hosts a unique website for speech pathologists. This site is a gathering place for speech professionals to exchange favorite strategies, ideas, and speech therapy tips. Drop by for a visit at http://www.tcsn.net/geezer/default.htm.

CHECK IT OUT

American Academy of Audiology
1735 North Lynn Street, Number 900
Arlington, Virginia 22209

American Association for Adult and Continuing Education
1200 19th Street NW, Suite 300
Washington, D.C. 20036

American Federation of Teachers
555 New Jersey Avenue NW
Washington, D.C. 20001

American Speech-Language-Hearing Association
10801 Rockville Pike
Rockville, Maryland 20852

American Vocational Association
1410 King Street
Alexandria, Virginia 22314

National Association for the Education of Young Children
1509 16th Street NW
Washington, D.C. 20036

National Community Education Association
119 North Payne Street
Alexandria, Virginia 22314

National Education Association
1201 16th Street NW
Washington, D.C. 20036

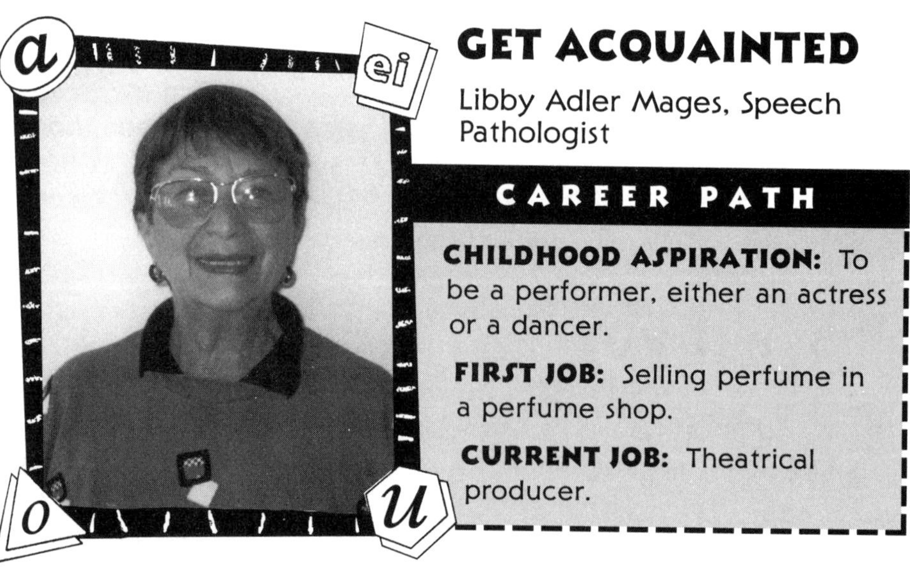

GET ACQUAINTED

Libby Adler Mages, Speech Pathologist

CAREER PATH

CHILDHOOD ASPIRATION: To be a performer, either an actress or a dancer.

FIRST JOB: Selling perfume in a perfume shop.

CURRENT JOB: Theatrical producer.

KIDS CAME FIRST

While in her 20s, Libby Adler Mages began her career as a speech pathologist because she wanted to work with children. She had a deep need to care for and help them overcome adversity in their daily lives. She spent many years enjoying this work.

When she had her own family, she accepted a position as a university speech teacher. She taught speech, voice and diction, and the foundations of speech. This job allowed her to multiply her impact because she was teaching others who would eventually go out and teach children.

She eventually became the associate head of her department and began to get more and more involved in the arts and drama. It was a natural outcome of her work with speech and speaking, even though she went from being in the sciences where everything was factual and orderly to being in the arts where everything was creative.

Mages' career path illustrates what can happen when you keep your options open.

BROADWAY BECKONS

Mages now spends her time producing theatrical plays all over the United States. One of the projects she's enjoyed most was developing a theatrical script for *Do Black Patent Leather Shoes Really Reflect Up?* She worked on the script and helped produce the play. It took over a year, but it was a big step toward what she does successfully today.

FOLLOW YOUR DREAM

Mages says that she got where she is today by following her dreams. She says the first step toward making a dream come true is having the courage to dream your own dream. She encourages young people to decide what they really want to do. Then, she says, give yourself a chance to try it out, think about it, and imagine yourself doing it.

Probably the most important parts of making dreams come true are believing that you can do it and working hard to make it happen. Most dreams don't get delivered on silver platters. You have to go for it!

Sports Professional

SKILL SET

- ✔ TALKING
- ✔ SPORTS
- ✔ BUSINESS

SHORTCUTS

GO take a class at a health and fitness club.

READ *Tiger Woods: A Biography* by Bill Gutman (New York: Pocket Books, 1997).

TRY teaching a friend how to play your favorite game.

WHAT IS A SPORTS PROFESSIONAL?

A successful sports professional, or pro, has to be good enough to wow seasoned athletes and patient enough to teach first-time players. Sports pros work at resorts or clubs and teach a particular sport such as golf, tennis, swimming, or skiing.

Sports pros can work with individuals or groups, children or adults. They must be able to instruct, evaluate, and advise both beginners and experts on ways to improve their game or skills. A training session with a sports pro generally consists of three parts: a demonstration of the required skills, an explanation of the rules, and an overview of basic safety precautions. After that it's practice, practice, and more practice on specific skills.

Communication skills and the ability to get along with others are just as important as athletic ability in this people-oriented business. Sports pros have to keep their students motivated to work hard and challenged to push themselves to improve.

Training other trainers is often part of the job for the more experienced sports pro. Other advanced opportunities for sports pros include running the administrative side of a training program or supervising other instructors.

Other types of sports such as diving, hiking, and cycling lend themselves to other types of ventures for sports pros (and fanatics). Organizing tours and special trips for beginners and more advanced learners is another way to earn a living by teaching others how to play.

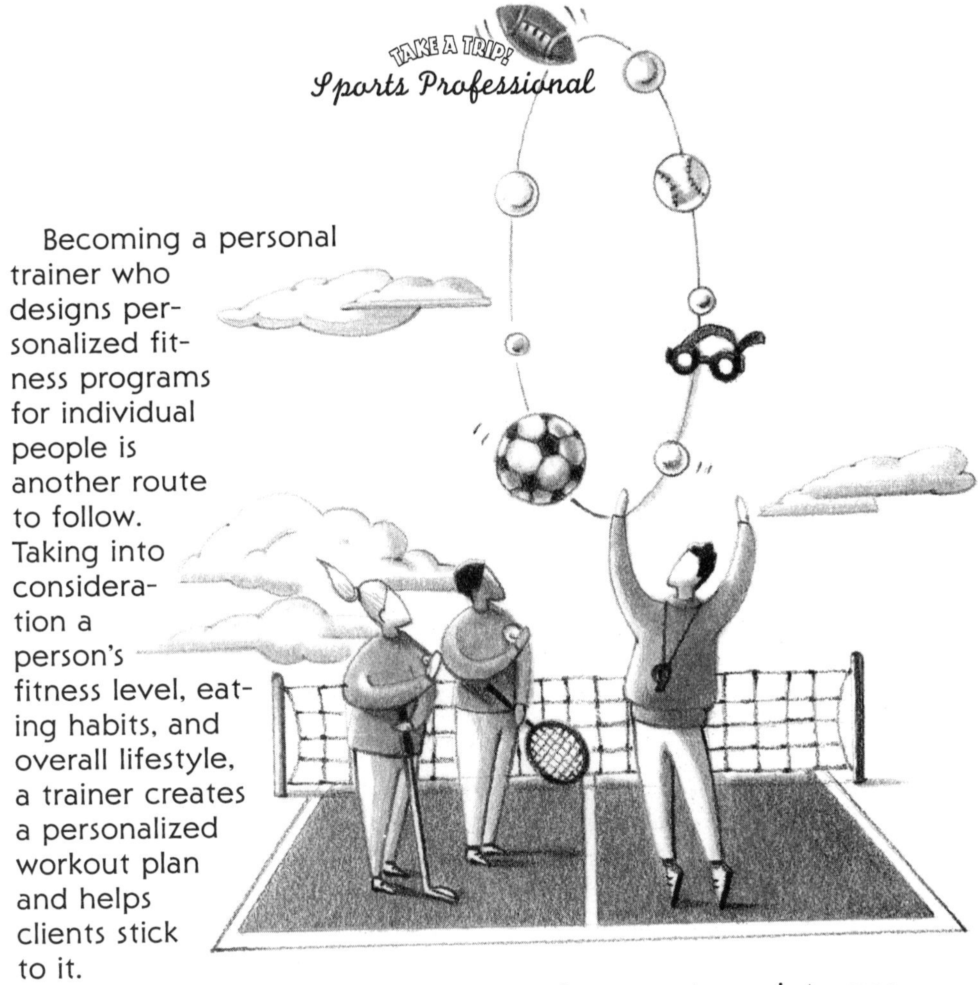

Becoming a personal trainer who designs personalized fitness programs for individual people is another route to follow. Taking into consideration a person's fitness level, eating habits, and overall lifestyle, a trainer creates a personalized workout plan and helps clients stick to it.

The best training anyone can get to be a sports pro is to master one's sport. Needless to say, a golf pro must be an excellent golfer, and a ski instructor must be a great skier. It is essential that sports pros have good communication skills, and it really helps if they genuinely enjoy working with people. Focus, concentration, and massive amounts of patience also come in handy when training other people.

TRY IT OUT

JOIN THE CLUB

The best advice for would-be sports pros: If your game is hockey, play hockey; if your sport is tennis, play tennis; etc. If your school has a team or club for any of these sports, join it. Learn all you can.

Remember, you have to be *very* good at your sport to be a sports pro. Enter tournaments and contests. Play the tour. The more you play, the better you get. The better you get, the easier it is to help others.

CLIMB THE LADDER OF SUCCESS

Not many junior high or senior high students can walk into a resort or country club and get a job as a sports pro. But they can walk in and get a job as a caddie, gift shop clerk, or dishwasher. Getting entry level jobs in places that also employ sports pros lets you start learning while you're earning. Watch how the pros work with people, observe their own practice sessions, and ask as many questions as you can.

WALKING SPORTS ENCYCLOPEDIA

Part of a sports pro's job is to keep students entertained. Since the pro and the student share a common interest in the sport, keep up with what's happening and who's doing what so that you'll always have plenty to talk about.

There are several ways to build your storehouse of knowledge. Read the sports section of newspapers and sports journals (*Sports Illustrated* is one of the best sources for comprehensive coverage of major sports). Watch sports broadcasts on the news and frequent cable channels like ESPN.

For the computer-literate, there are a growing number of information resources and forums on the Internet. Following are addresses for a few general sources.

- http://www.cnnsi.com
- http://sfgate.com/sports/
- http://tns-www.lcs.mit.edu/cgi-bin/sports

In addition, there are dozens of sites catering to even the most remote sports. Use a search engine to track down information on your favorites.

COPYCAT

As the saying goes, "Imitation is the sincerest form of flattery." While you may have to face the fact that you'll never be the next Michael Jordan or Tiger Woods, you can learn to apply some of their best traits to your own sports career.

First, make a list of your favorite sports heroes. Leave space for comments under each name. Next, think about the traits that make these people so successful. Is it their focus? Their persistence and dedication? Finally, describe these special traits in the space beneath each name. Determine to do whatever it takes to be a copycat in some of these important areas.

CHECK IT OUT

American Alliance for
Health, Physical Education,
Recreation and Dance
1900 Association Drive
Reston, Virginia 22091

Athletic Institute
200 Castlewood Drive
North Palm Beach, Florida
33408

Ladies Professional Golfers
Association
2570 West International
Speedway Boulevard,
Suite B
Dayton, Florida 32114

National Athletic Trainers
Association
2952 Stemmons Freeway
Dallas, Texas 75247-6103

National PGA Tour Office
TPC Sawgrass
Ponte Vedra, Florida 32082

National Professional Golfers
of America
100 Avenue of the Champions
Palm Beach Gardens, Florida
33410
800-474-2776

Professional Ski Instructors of
America
1323 S. Van Gordon, Suite 101
Lakewood, Colorado 80228

U.S. Golf Association
Liberty Corner
Far Hills, New Jersey 07937

U.S. Tennis Association
70 West Red Oak Lane
White Plains, New York 10604

GET ACQUAINTED

Scott Moore, Golf Professional

CAREER PATH

CHILDHOOD ASPIRATION: To be a PGA tour professional.

FIRST JOB: Caddie, ball shagger, golf course grass cutter.

CURRENT JOB: Golf professional.

HE GETS PAID TO HAVE FUN

Scott Moore loves to play golf. It's been a passion of his since he was old enough to walk around the golf course. His dad was a golf pro, so Moore spent much of his childhood shagging balls and caddying. He learned the sport at an early age, and he lives and breathes it now. Sometimes he has to pinch himself to believe that he earns his living playing golf.

PEE-WEE SPECIAL

One of the most rewarding parts of his job is working with children, especially those who have never even seen a golf course before. Every Tuesday afternoon at 2:00, Moore introduces a new bunch of kids to the game. It's nice to see a child's face light up when he or she makes a good shot. He says some children are natural golfers, and he enjoys being part of turning them on to the sport.

A SPECIAL PERK OF THE JOB

The most treasured part of his job is the lifelong friendships that he's cultivated with many of his clients. Mutual trust is an important part of these special relationships.

In the course of an 18-hole game, there's plenty of time to talk. His clients often share details about their marriages, their kids, their problems, and their hopes and dreams. He says he keeps things confidential and doesn't tell secrets. He likes being a sort of sounding board for ideas and feelings, as well as teaching a good game of golf.

IT'S A DEAL

Golf is a favorite sport of businesspeople everywhere. He says that sometimes he feels like a fly on the wall watching a big business deal come together during a round of golf. The give-and-take process can make for an interesting game.

WILDEST DREAMS

Moore never thought that he could go from being a golf pro at 24 years old to owning his own golf course at 34. But that's just what he's done. In the process, he's added financing, inventory control, marketing, and personnel management to his job description. In spite of a few nightmarish aspects in the process, it's been a dream come true.

A FAMILY AFFAIR

Moore says that if he didn't have the support of his family, he wouldn't be able to do his job. He works long hours. He often leaves the house before his young children are up in the morning and doesn't get home until after they're in bed. His busiest times at work are during their school vacations and on weekends.

He makes a special effort to set time aside to be with his family. This helps. But, it's nice to know they're behind him 100 percent.

FREE ADVICE

Moore has a few tips to help you improve your chances of success as a sports pro.

- Be prepared to put in long hours. (During the off-season he still works 50-hour weeks at his Alabama golf course.)
- Be prepared to really love what you do.
- Be patient. Some people gripe about everything and you'll have a difficult time pleasing everyone. But you'll make some great contacts.

Telemarketer

SKILL SET

✔ BUSINESS
✔ COMPUTERS
✔ TALKING

SHORTCUTS

GO browse through the telephone equipment at an office supply store to see the newest kinds of gizmos available.

READ *Life's a Pitch . . . & Then You Buy* by Don Peppers (New York: Doubleday, 1995).

TRY calling people in your school to remind them about a meeting or an assignment.

WHAT ARE TELEMARKETERS?

The invention of the telephone completely revolutionized the way people do business. With recent advances in modems, faxes, and e-mail, the telephone continues to have a major impact on all kinds of business.

A telemarketer typically calls hundreds of people every day in order to sell products and services over the phone. Telemarketers are used to get information to or from a group of people quickly and efficiently. Often automatic dialing systems are used. As soon as one call is done, the computer automatically dials another. So, it can mean constant (make that nonstop) telephone talking.

Telephones are so important to business that there are a number of specific telemarketing careers that revolve around using them almost exclusively.

Airline reservation agents work for a specific airline and help customers book flights. Using sophisticated computer programs, they check on the status of a flight, make seat assignments, and issue tickets.

A collection agent calls people who haven't paid their bills on time. His or her mission is to collect the money owed to the client. Contrary to popular opinion, these agents don't use strong-arm tactics to do this, just the telephone. They need to be firm with people and comfortable about asking for money. They can't take flimsy excuses or "no" for an answer.

There are several different kinds of dispatchers. One kind uses a telephone and a radio to make sure that taxis, rental trucks, trains, and other forms of ground transportation get to where they need to go. A police dispatcher will take emergency calls and relay them to the officers responding to each situation. An emergency (911) dispatcher might also send an ambulance, a fire crew, or a helicopter to the scene of an accident.

A customer service representative uses the telephone to talk to customers of a business. Representatives may fill orders or deal with complaints. Either way, they use the phone to keep customers happy.

A hotel desk clerk takes reservations from people calling in, directs calls from guests to the correct person, and forwards incoming calls to guests. Like a receptionist, the desk clerk is often a first contact with the hotel for some people. He or she may also be the person who processes guests in and out of the hotel.

A market researcher gathers information about products, lifestyles, habits, and choices—really just about anything anyone wants to know. A market researcher might make calls to find out how someone is likely to vote in the next election, what radio station they listen to, or what kind of soap they use in the laundry. The information that is gathered is compiled into reports that are used to help business leaders make decisions. For instance, if the information indicates that nobody is listening to their radio station, the company president would want to make some big changes.

A receptionist answers calls that come into an office and directs calls to the appropriate person or department. This may sound easy, but when you are answering 100

or more phone lines at once, it can get pretty hectic. Receptionists are usually stationed at the main entrance to the building so that they can also greet visitors as they arrive for meetings. Whether over the phone or in person, the receptionist is often the first contact people have with a business—and first impressions make lasting impressions of the company.

Securities brokers spend time on the phone talking to investors and gathering information about stock offerings and other trading information. They may also provide financial counseling or help people with investment buying decisions or insurance purchases. This job requires some extensive training and, in most cases, a college degree.

The telephone company uses telephone operators to give out information and telephone numbers or to make international telephone and collect call connections.

A travel agent helps customers plan trips—either for business or for pleasure. Agents make reservations on behalf of customers with airlines, hotels, rental car agencies, tour facilities, and other places around the world. Getting a person or an organization from point A to point B can require some clever logistical maneuvering.

TRY IT OUT

TALK IT UP

There are many organizations that would be glad to put your budding (and semiprofessional) telephone skills to work. Contact a favorite charity or nonprofit organization or a political candidate you admire. Ask if they need any help on the phones. You may have to take a training class or memorize a prepared script before making calls. This can be a great way to do some good while learning new skills.

TAKE A SURVEY

Ever wondered what all your friends think about your school? Take a survey. First, make up a list of questions to ask. Then, put together a script. Practice it and rework it until it comes across in a natural way.

Call each student in your class and ask them to complete the survey. After you've called everyone, tally up the answers and write an article for the school newspaper about the results.

CHECK IT OUT

American Train Dispatchers Association
1370 Ontario Street
Cleveland, Ohio 44113

Associated Public Safety Communications Officers
2040 South Ridgewood
South Daytona, Florida 32119-8437

Communication Workers of America
Research Department
501 Third Street NW
Washington, D.C. 20001

The Educational Institute of the American Hotel and Motel Association
P.O. Box 1240
East Lansing, Michigan 48826-1240

Make-A-Wish Foundation
2600 North Central Avenue
Phoenix, Arizona 85004
800-722-9474

Manufacturers' Agents National Association
P.O. Box 3467
Laguna Hills, California 92654-3467

United States Telephone Association
1401 H Street NW, Suite 600
Washington, D.C. 20005-2136

GET ACQUAINTED

Tim Stiers, Telemarketer

CAREER PATH

CHILDHOOD ASPIRATION: To find any career that would make lots of money.

FIRST JOB: Cutting grass during the summer.

CURRENT JOB: Fund-raiser for a national promotional company.

DIAL AND SMILE

Tim Stiers spends his time calling people to raise money for various charities and nonprofit groups. Using the phone allows him to reach more people and raise more money than if he used the mail or other means of making contact with the people who want to make a contribution.

He generally spends about 15 seconds talking about the charity and another 15 seconds to make the sale—30 to 45 seconds in all. If it takes him only 15 seconds to make the initial connection, he can make lots of calls in a single day. In fact, he says he will dial more than 700 numbers each day. Only some of them actually go through, but he still talks to a lot of people and manages to raise quite a bit of money each day for the charities he works for.

CELEBRITY PERKS

Stiers loves doing special promotions for favorite charities. Often a big charity will put on a concert or other special event to raise money. He organized a charity concert by recording artist Charlie Daniels in Michigan that sold out the arena where it was held. It took Stiers six months to put the whole event together, but the place was packed the night of the concert. He got to meet Charlie Daniels, go backstage, talk to the press and the promoters, and see the band up close. That event raised almost half a million dollars for the charity, and people got to see a great show in the process.

Stiers says that's one of the best perks to his job—meeting the celebrities. But, he says the people he calls are the real celebrities. They make a difference in people's lives through their contributions.

REJECTION IS OK

The very nature of the job means that Stiers gets lots of turndowns and rejections. Some people can be rude on the phone. You have to be pretty thick-skinned to handle it. Stiers likes to think of a rejection as a statistic. He knows he will get so many rejections for every sale he makes. So, each rejection is just one step closer to the call that will make the sale. He focuses on the people he calls and the fact that he's working for a good cause.

HOW DO YOU DEFINE SUCCESS?

For Stiers, defining his own idea of success was important. He started doing this type of work because he needed to feed his family. It was an easy job to get into, and he was concerned about providing for his family's future.

His boss helped him learn the ropes and get through the early rejections. It didn't take long before he began to make sales and meet his goals, so he set new ones. Over time his confidence grew.

MAKE A VERBAL DETOUR!

The preceding career highlights have introduced many fascinating options for people who love to talk. But since the general idea here is to explore *all* your options, here's a list of more careers. There are probably at least three you've never heard of before. Look them up at the library, perhaps starting with the career encyclopedias listed on page 148. Get acquainted with more possibilities for your future!

A WORLD OF TALKING CAREERS

IN THE PEOPLE BUSINESS

In one way or another the following careers revolve around people. Most involve using communication skills as a way to help people overcome problems and make positive changes in their lives.

adolescent-care technician
adolescent chemical-dependency counselor
affirmative action officer
alcohol counselor/alcoholism counselor
case manager
chemical dependency advocate/coordinator/technician
community activist
consumer credit counselor
corrections officer
divorce mediator
funeral director
group-home parent
home health aide
marriage counselor
psychologist
vocational counselor

TALKING MAKES THE WORLD GO 'ROUND

The business world revolves around effective communication skills. Find an idea that you like from the following sampling and talk your way into a good career.

advertising executive
arbitration specialist
attorney/lawyer
auctioneer
bank teller
building inspector
conference planner
consultant
consumer advocate
conference planner
editor
human-relations director
information-referral specialist

LET'S TALK ABOUT EDUCATION

When it comes right down to it, teaching anyone any skill boils down to telling what you know. These careers represent the many opportunities that are involved in educating people young and old.

admissions representative
child-care provider
coach
college professor
driving instructor
early childhood education specialist
interpreter
librarian
linguist
school administrator
teacher
tutor

UNCLE SAM NEEDS YOU

Government service offers a wide variety of opportunities for public servants blessed with the gift of gab. Among the opportunities are:

census worker
diplomat
military drill instructor
postal worker
public information officer

A LITTLE OF THIS, A LITTLE OF THAT

Once you start looking, you'll find opportunities for big talkers everywhere you look. There's plenty of room for having fun and lots of ways to be creative in piecing together a career that works for you. Some of these ideas provide ample room for starting out with little or no experience or advanced education and working your way up. How about waitress today and CEO of a chain of restaurants tomorrow?

bridal consultant
bus driver
car rental agent
circus ringleader
comedian
concierge
cosmetologist
cruise director
docent
entertainer
event coordinator
lifeguard
party planner
personal shopper
restaurant manager
storyteller
tour guide
waitress or waiter

INFORMATION IS POWER

Mind-boggling, isn't it? There are so many great choices, so many jobs you've never heard of before. How will you ever narrow it down to the perfect spot for you?

First, pinpoint the ideas that sound the most interesting to you. Then, find out all you can about them. As you may have noticed, a similar pattern of information was used for each of the career entries included in this book. Each entry included

- a general description or definition of the career
- some hands-on projects that give readers a chance to actually experience a job
- a list of organizations to contact for more information
- an interview with a professional

You can use information like this to help you determine the best career path to pursue. Since there isn't room in one book to profile all these verbal career choices, here's your chance to do it yourself. Conduct a full investigation into a talking career that interests you.

Please Note: If this book does not belong to you use a separate sheet of paper to record your responses to the following questions.

CAREER TITLE ______________________

WHAT IS A ______________________**?**

Use career encyclopedias and other resources to write a description of this career.

____
____
____

SKILL SET

✔ __________
✔ __________
✔ __________

TRY IT OUT

Write project ideas here. Ask your parents and your teacher to come up with a plan.

____
____
____

CHECK IT OUT

List professional organizations where you can learn more about this profession.

____
____
____

GET ACQUAINTED

Interview a professional in the field and summarize your findings.

____
____
____

It's been a fast-paced trip so far. Take a break, regroup, and look at all the progress you've made.

1st Stop: Self-Discovery
You discovered some personal interests and natural abilities that you can start building a career around.

2nd Stop: Exploration
You've explored an exciting array of career opportunities in talking. You're now aware that your career can involve either a specialized area with many educational requirements or that it can involve a practical application of communication methods with a minimum of training and experience.

At this point, you've found a couple of (or few) careers that really intrigue you. Now it's time to put it all together and do all you can to make an informed, intelligent choice. It's time to move on.

3rd Stop: Experimentation

By the time you finish this section, you'll have reached one of three points in the career planning process.

1. **Green light!** You found it. No need to look any further. This is *the* career for you. (This may happen to a lucky few. Don't worry if it hasn't happened yet for you. This whole process is about exploring options, experimenting with ideas, and, eventually, making the best choice for you.)
2. **Yellow light!** Close, but not quite. You seem to be on the right path but you haven't nailed things down for sure. (This is where many people your age end up, and it's a good place to be. You've learned what it takes to really check things out. Hang in there. Your time will come.)
3. **Red light!** Whoa! No doubt about it, this career just isn't for you. (Congratulations! Aren't you glad you found out now and not after you'd spent four years in college preparing for this career? Your next stop: Make a U-turn and start this process over with another career.)

Here's a sneak peek at what you'll be doing in the next section.

- First, you'll pick a favorite career idea (or two or three).
- Second, you'll snoop around the library to find answers to the 10 things you've just got to know about your future career.
- Third, you'll pick up the phone and talk to someone whose career you admire to find out what it's really like.
- Fourth, you'll link up with a whole world of great information about your career idea on the Internet (it's easier than you think).
- Fifth, you'll go on the job to shadow a professional for a day.

Hang on to your hats and get ready to make tracks!

#1 NARROW DOWN YOUR CHOICES

You've been introduced to quite a few talking career ideas. You may also have some ideas of your own to add. Which ones appeal to you the most?

Write your top three choices in the spaces below. (Sorry if this is starting to sound like a broken record, but . . . if this book does not belong to you, write your responses on a separate sheet of paper.)

1. ______________________________
2. ______________________________
3. ______________________________

#2 SNOOP AT THE LIBRARY

Take your list of favorite career ideas, a notebook, and a helpful adult with you to the library. When you get there, go to the reference section and ask the librarian to help you find books about careers. Most libraries will have at least one set of career encyclopedias. Some of the larger libraries may also have career information on CD-ROM.

Gather all the information you can and use it to answer the following questions in your notebook about each of the careers on your list. Make sure to ask for help if you get stuck.

TOP 10 THINGS YOU NEED TO KNOW ABOUT YOUR CAREER

1. What kinds of skills does this job require?
2. What kind of training is required? (Compare the options for a high school degree, trade school degree, two-year degree, four-year degree, and advanced degree.)
3. What types of classes do I need to take in high school in order to be accepted into a training program?
4. What are the names of three schools or colleges where I can get the training I need?
5. Are there any apprenticeship or internship opportunities available? If so, where? If not, could I create my own opportunity? How?
6. How much money can I expect to earn as a beginner? How much with more experience?
7. What kinds of places hire people to do this kind of work?
8. What is a typical work environment like? For example, would I work in a busy office, outdoors, or in a laboratory?
9. What are some books and magazines I could read to learn more about this career? Make a list and look for them at your library.
10. Where can I write for more information? Make a list of professional associations.

#3 CHAT ON THE PHONE

Talking to a seasoned professional—someone who experiences the job day in and day out—can be a great way to get the inside story on what a career is all about. Fortunately for you, the experts in any career field can be as close as the nearest telephone.

Sure it can be a bit scary calling up an adult whom you don't know. But, two things are in your favor:

1. They can't see you. The worst thing they can do is hang up on you, so just relax and enjoy the conversation.
2. They'll probably be happy to talk to you about their job. In fact, most people will be flattered that you've called. If you happen to contact someone who seems reluctant to talk, thank them for their time and try someone else.

Here are a few pointers to help make your telephone interview a success.

- Mind your manners and speak clearly.
- Be respectful of their time and position.
- Be prepared with good questions and take notes as you talk.

One more common sense reminder: Be careful about giving out your address and DO NOT arrange to meet anyone you don't know without your parents' supervision.

TRACKING DOWN CAREER EXPERTS

You might be wondering by now how to find someone to interview. Have no fear! It's easy, if you're persistent. All you have to do is ask. Ask the right people and you'll have a great lead in no time.

A few of the people to ask and sources to turn to are

Your parents. They may know someone (or know someone who knows someone) who has just the kind of job you're looking for.

Your friends and neighbors. You might be surprised to find out how many interesting jobs these people have when you start asking them what they (or their parents) do for a living.

Librarians. Since you've already figured out what kinds of companies employ people in your field of interest, the next step is to ask for information about local employers. Although it's a bit cumbersome to use, a big volume called *Contacts Influential* can provide this kind of information.

Professional associations. Call or write to the professional associations you discovered in Activity #1 a few pages back and ask for recommendations.

Chambers of commerce. The local chamber of commerce probably has a directory of employers, their specialties, and their phone numbers. Call the chamber, explain what you are looking for, and give them a chance to help their future workforce.

Newspaper and magazine articles. Find an article about the subject you are interested in. Chances are pretty good that it will mention the name of at least one expert in the field. The article probably won't include the person's phone number (that would be too easy), so you'll have to look for clues. Common clues include the name of the company that they work for, the town that they live in, and if the person is an author, the name of their publisher. Make a few phone calls and track them down (if long distance calls are involved, make sure to get your parents' permission first).

INQUIRING KIDS WANT TO KNOW

Before you make the call, make a list of questions to ask. You'll cover more ground if you focus on using the five w's (and the h) that you've probably heard about in your creative writing classes: Who? What? Where? When? How? and Why? For example,

1. Who do you work for?
2. What is a typical work day like for you?
3. Where can I get some on-the-job experience?
4. When did you become a ______________________ ?
   (profession)
5. How much can you earn in this profession? (But, remember it's not polite to ask someone how much *he* or *she* earns.)
6. Why did you choose this profession?

One last suggestion: Add a professional (and very classy) touch to the interview process by following up with a thank-you note to the person who took time out of a busy schedule to talk with you.

#4 SURF THE NET

With the Internet, the new information superhighway, charging full steam ahead, you literally have a world of information at your fingertips. The Internet has something for everyone, and it's getting easier to access all the time. An increasing number of libraries and schools are offering access to the Internet on their computers. In addition, companies such as America Online and CompuServe have made it possible for anyone with a home computer to surf the World Wide Web.

A typical career search will land everything from the latest news on developments in the field and course notes from universities to museum exhibits, interactive games, educational activities, and more. You just can't beat the timeliness or the variety of information available on the Net.

One of the easiest ways to track down this information is to use an Internet search engine, such as Yahoo! Simply type in the topic you are looking for, and in a matter of seconds, you'll have a list of options from around the world. It's fun to browse—you never know what you'll come up with.

To narrow down your search a bit, look for specific websites, forums, or chatrooms that are related to your topic in the following publications:

Hahn, Harley. *The Internet Yellow Pages.* Berkeley, Calif.: Osborne McGraw Hill, 1997.

———. *The World Wide Web Yellow Pages.* Berkeley, Calif.: Osborne McGraw Hill, 1997.

To go on-line at home you may want to compare two of the more popular on-line services: America Online and CompuServe. Please note that there is a monthly subscription fee for using these services. There can also be extra fees attached to specific forums and services, so *make sure you have your parents' OK before you sign up.* For information about America Online call 800-827-6364. For information about CompuServe call 800-848-8990. Both services frequently offer free start-up deals, so shop around.

There are also many other services, depending on where you live. Check your local phone book or ads in local computer magazines for other service options.

Before you link up, keep in mind that many of these sites are geared toward professionals who are already working in a particular field. Some of the sites can get pretty technical. Just use the experience as a chance to nose around the field, hang out with the people who are tops in the field, and think about whether or not you'd like to be involved in a profession like that.

Specific sites to look for are the following:

Professional associations. Find out about what's happening in the field, conferences, journals, and other helpful tidbits.

Schools that specialize in this area. Many include research tools, introductory courses, and all kinds of interesting information.

Government agencies. Quite a few are going high-tech with lots of helpful resources.

Websites hosted by experts in the field (this seems to be a popular hobby among many professionals). These websites are often as entertaining as they are informative.

If you're not sure where to go, just start clicking around. Sites often link to other sites. You may want to jot down notes about favorite sites. Sometimes you can even print out information that isn't copyright-protected; try the print option and see what happens.

Be prepared: Surfing the Internet can be an addicting habit! There is so much awesome information. It's a fun way to focus on your future.

#5 SHADOW A PROFESSIONAL

Linking up with someone who is gainfully employed in a profession that you want to explore is a great way to find out what a career is like. Following someone around while they are at work is called "shadowing." Try it!

This process involves three steps.

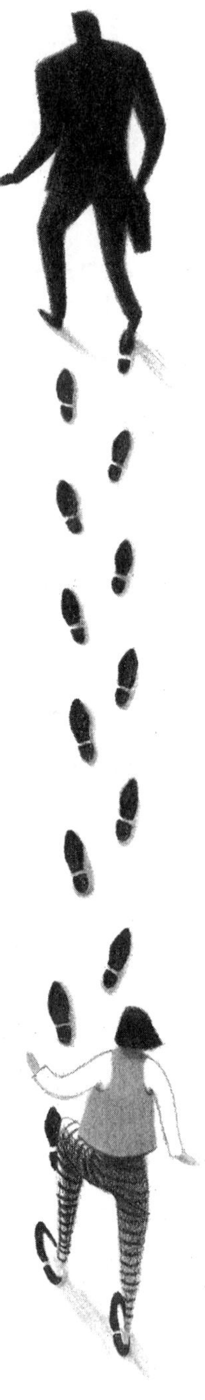

1. Find someone to shadow. Some suggestions include
   - the person you interviewed (if you enjoyed talking with them and feel comfortable about asking them to show you around their workplace)
   - friends and neighbors (you may even be shocked to discover that your parents have interesting jobs)
   - workers at the chamber of commerce may know of mentoring programs available in your area (it's a popular concept, so most larger areas should have something going on)
   - someone at your local School-to-Work office, the local Boy Scouts Explorer program director (this is available to girls too!), or your school guidance counselor
2. Make a date. Call and make an appointment. Find out when is the best time for arrival and departure. Make arrangements with a parent or other respected adult to go with you and get there on time.
3. Keep your ears and eyes open. This is one time when it is OK to be nosy. Ask questions. Notice everything that is happening around you. Ask your host to let you try some of the tasks he or she is doing.

The basic idea of the shadowing experience is to put yourself in the other person's shoes and see how they fit. Imagine yourself having a job like this 10 or 15 years down the road. It's a great way to find out if you are suited for a particular line of work.

BE CAREFUL OUT THERE!

Two cautions must accompany this recommendation. First, remember the stranger danger rules of your childhood. NEVER meet with anyone you don't know without your parents' permission and ALWAYS meet in a supervised situation—at the office or with your parents.

Second, be careful not to overdo it. These people are busy earning a living, so respect their time by limiting your contact and coming prepared with valid questions and background information.

PLAN B

If shadowing opportunities are limited where you live, try one of these approaches for learning the ropes from a professional.

Pen pals. Find a mentor who is willing to share information, send interesting materials, or answer specific questions that come up during your search.

Cyber pals. Go on-line in a forum or chatroom related to your profession. You'll be able to chat with professionals from all over the world.

If you want to get some more on-the-job experience, try one of these approaches.

Volunteer to do the dirty work. Volunteer to work for someone who has a job that interests you for a specified period of time. Do anything—filing, errands, emptying trash cans—that puts you in contact with professionals. Notice every tiny detail about the profession. Listen to the lingo they use in the profession. Watch how they perform their jobs on a day-to-day basis.

Be an apprentice. This centuries-old job training method is making a comeback. Find out if you can set up an official on-the-job training program to gain valuable experi-

ence. Ask professional associations about apprenticeship opportunities. Once again, a School-to-Work program can be a great asset. In many areas, they've established some very interesting career training opportunities.

Hire yourself for the job. Maybe you are simply too young to do much in the way of on-the-job training right now. That's OK. Start learning all you can now and you'll be ready to really wow them when the time is right. Make sure you do all the Try It Out activities included for the career(s) you are most interested in. Use those activities as a starting point for creating other projects that will give you a feel for what the job is like.

Have you carefully worked your way through all of the suggested activities? You haven't tried to sneak past anything, have you? This isn't a place for shortcuts. If you've done the activities, you're ready to decide where you stand with each career idea. So what is it? Green light? See page 140. Yellow light? See page 139. Red light? See page 138. Find the spot that best describes your response to what you've discovered about this career idea and plan your next move.

RED LIGHT

So you've decided this career is definitely not for you—hang in there! The process of elimination is an important one. You've learned some valuable career planning skills; use them to explore other ideas. In the meantime, use the following road map to chart a plan to get beyond this "spinning your wheels" point in the process.

Take a variety of classes at school to expose yourself to new ideas and expand the options. Make a list of courses you want to try.

- ____
- ____
- ____
- ____

Get involved in clubs and other after-school activities (like 4-H or Boy Scout Explorer's) to further develop your interests. Write down some that interest you.

- ____
- ____
- ____
- ____

Read all you can find about interesting people and their work. Make a list of people you'd like to learn more about.

- ____
- ____
- ____
- ____

Keep at it. Time is on your side. Finding the perfect work for you is worth a little effort. Once you've crossed this hurdle, move on to the next pages and continue mapping out a great future.

YELLOW LIGHT

Proceed with caution. While the idea continues to intrigue you, you may wonder if it's the best choice for you. Your concerns are legitimate (listen to that nagging little voice inside!).

Maybe it's the training requirements that intimidate you. Maybe you have concerns about finding a good job once you complete the training. Maybe you wonder if you have what it takes to do the job.

At this point, it's good to remember that there is often more than one way to get somewhere. Check out all the choices and choose the route that's best for you. Use the following road map to move on down the road in your career planning adventure.

Make two lists. On the first, list the things you like most about the career you are currently investigating. On the second, list the things that are most important to you in a future career. Look for similarities on both lists and focus on careers that emphasize these similar key points.

Current Career	Future Career
______________	______________
______________	______________

What are some career ideas that are similar to the one you have in mind? Find out all you can about them. Go back through the exploration process explained on pages 127 to 136 and repeat some of the exercises that were most valuable.

- ______________________________
- ______________________________
- ______________________________
- ______________________________

Visit your school counselor and ask him or her which career assessment tools are available through your school. Use these to find out more about your strengths and interests. List the date, time, and place for any assessment tests you plan to take.

- ______
- ______
- ______
- ______

What other adults do you know and respect to whom you can talk about your future? They may have ideas that you've never thought of.

- ______
- ______
- ______
- ______

What kinds of part-time jobs, volunteer work, or after-school experiences can you look into that will give you a chance to build your skills and test your abilities? Think about how you can tap into these opportunities.

- ______
- ______
- ______
- ______

GREEN LIGHT

Yahoo! You are totally turned on to this career idea and ready to do whatever it takes to make it your life's work. Go for it!

Find out what kinds of classes you need to take now to prepare for this career. List them here.

- ______
- ______
- ______
- ______

What are some on-the-job training possibilities for you to pursue? List the company name, a person to contact and their phone number.

- ______________________________
- ______________________________
- ______________________________
- ______________________________

Find out if there are any internship or apprenticeship opportunities available in this career field. List contacts and phone numbers.

- ______________________________
- ______________________________
- ______________________________
- ______________________________

What kind of education will you need after you graduate from high school? Describe the options.

- ______________________________
- ______________________________
- ______________________________
- ______________________________

No matter what the educational requirements are, the better your grades are during junior and senior high school, the better your chances for the future.

Take a minute to think about some areas that need improvement in your school work. Write your goals for giving it all you've got here.

- ______________________________
- ______________________________
- ______________________________
- ______________________________

Where can you get the training you'll need? Make a list of colleges, technical schools, or vocational programs. Include addresses so that you can write to request a catalog.

- ______________________________
- ______________________________
- ______________________________
- ______________________________

HOORAY! YOU DID IT!

This has been quite a trip. If someone tries to tell you that this process is easy, don't believe them. Figuring out what you want to do with the rest of your life is heavy stuff, and it should be. If you don't put some thought (and some sweat and hard work) into the process, you'll get stuck with whatever comes your way.

You may not have things planned to a T. Actually, it's probably better if you don't. You'll change some of your ideas as you grow and experience new things. And, you may find an interesting detour or two along the way. That's OK.

The most important thing about beginning this process now is that you've started to dream. You've discovered that you have some unique talents and abilities to share. You've become aware of some of the ways you can use them to make a living—and, perhaps, make a difference in the world.

Whatever you do, don't lose sight of the hopes and dreams you've discovered. You've got your entire future ahead of you. Use it wisely.

SOME FUTURE DESTINATIONS

Wow! You've really made tracks during this whole process. Now that you've gotten this far, you'll want to keep moving forward to a great future. This section will point you toward some useful resources to help you make a conscientious career choice (that's just the opposite of falling into any old job on a fluke).

IT'S NOT JUST FOR NERDS

The school counselor's office is not just a place where teachers send troublemakers. One of its main purposes is to help students like you make the most of your educational opportunities. Most schools will have a number of useful resources, including career assessment tools (ask about the Self-Directed Search Career Explorer or the COPS Interest

Inventory—these are especially useful assessments for people your age). They may also have a stash of books, videos, and other helpful materials.

Make sure no one's looking and sneak into your school counseling office to get some expert advice!

AWESOME INTERNET CAREER RESOURCES

Your parents will be green with envy when they see all the career planning resources you have at your fingertips. Get ready to hear them whine, "But they didn't have all this stuff when I was kid." Make the most of these cyberspace opportunities.

- The Career Center for Teens (a site sponsored by Public Television Outreach) includes activities and information on 21st-century career opportunities. Find it at http://www.pbs.org/jobs/teenindex.html.
- Future Scan includes in-depth profiles on a wide variety of career choices and expert advice from their "Guidance Gurus." Check it out at http://www.futurescan.com.
- Just for fun visit the Jam!z Knowzone Careers page and chat with other kids about your career dreams. You'll find them by going to http://www.jamz.com and clicking on the KnowZone icon. (Behave yourself; it's monitored!)
- JobSmart's Career Guides is another site to explore specific career choices. Look for it at http://www.jobsmart.org/tools/career/spec-car.htm.

IT'S NOT JUST FOR BOYS

Boys and girls alike are encouraged to contact their local version of the Boy Scouts Explorer program. It offers exciting on-the-job training experiences in a variety of professional fields. Look in the white pages of your community phone book for the local Boy Scouts of America program.

MORE CAREER BOOKS ESPECIALLY FOR BIG TALKERS

Communications is a field that offers more opportunity than a single book can contain. Keep looking for the perfect fit for your talking ambitions. Start with some of the following books.

Allessandra, Tony, and Phil Hunsaker. *Communicating at Work.* New York: Simon and Schuster, 1993.

Camerson, Blythe. *Great Jobs for Communications Majors.* Lincolnwood, Ill.: VGM, 1995.

Camerson, Blythe, and Jan Goldberg. *Real People Working in Communications.* Lincolnwood, Ill.: VGM, 1996.

Career Associates. *Career Choices for Students of Political Science and Government.* New York: Walker, 1990.

Career Information Center. *Hospitality and Recreation.* New York: Macmillan, 1996.

Goldberg, Jan. *Careers in Journalism.* Lincolnwood, Ill.: VGM, 1995.

Meyer, Scott A. *100 Jobs in Words.* New York: Macmillan, 1995.

Schloff, Laurie, and Marcia Yudkow. *Smart Speaking: Sixty-Second Strategies.* New York: Henry Holt, 1991.

Tanner, Deborah. *Talking from 9 to 5.* New York: William Morrow, 1994.

Tingley, Judith C. *Say What You Mean, Get What You Want.* New York: AMACOM, 1996.

In addition to these books, an entire series called Opportunities in Communication Careers is available from VGM. Here are some specific titles.

Bone, Jan. *Cable Television.* Lincolnwood, Ill.: VGM, 1993.

———. *Telecommunications.* Lincolnwood, Ill.: VGM, 1995.

Carter, Robert A. *Book Publishing.* Lincolnwood, Ill.: VGM, 1995.

———. *Publishing.* Lincolnwood, Ill.: VGM, 1995.

Deen, Robert. *Business Communications.* Lincolnwood, Ill.: VGM, 1987.

Ellis, Elmo I. *Broadcasting.* Lincolnwood, Ill.: VGM, 1992.

Ferguson, Donald L. *Journalism.* Lincolnwood, Ill.: VGM, 1993.

Foote-Smith, Elizabeth. *Writing.* Lincolnwood, Ill.: VGM, 1989.
Gould, Jay. *Technical Writing and Communications.* Lincolnwood, Ill.: VGM, 1994.
Noronha, Shonan. *Television and Video.* Lincolnwood, Ill.: VGM, 1993.
Pattis, William S. *Advertising.* Lincolnwood, Ill.: VGM, 1995.
Rivers, Wilga A. *Foreign Language.* Lincolnwood, Ill.: VGM, 1993.
Rotman, Morris B. *Public Relations.* Lincolnwood, Ill.: VGM, 1995.
Tebbel, John. *Newspaper Publishing.* Lincolnwood, Ill.: VGM, 1989.

HEAVY-DUTY RESOURCES

Career encyclopedias provide general information about a lot of professions and can be a great place to start a career search. Those listed here are easy to use and provide useful information about nearly a zillion different jobs. Look for them in the reference section of your local library.

Cosgrove, Holli, ed. *Career Discovery Encyclopedia: 1997 Edition.* Chicago: J. G. Ferguson Publishing Company, 1997.
Encyclopedia of Career Choices for the 1990's. New York: Perigee Books/Putnam Publishing Group, 1992.
Maze, Marilyn, Donald Mayall, and J. Michael Farr. *The Enhanced Guide for Occupational Exploration: Descriptions for the 2,500 Most Important Jobs.* Indianapolis: JIST, 1991.
VGM's Careers Encyclopedia. Lincolnwood, Ill.: VGM Career Books, 1991.

FINDING PLACES TO WORK

Use resources like these to find leads on local businesses, mentors, job shadowing opportunities, and internships. Later, use these same resources to find a great job!

Lanthrop, Richard. *Who's Hiring Who?* Berkeley, Calif.: Ten Speed Press, 1989.

LeCompte, Michelle. *Job Hunter's Sourcebook: Where to Find Employment Leads and Other Job Search Resources.* Detroit: Gale Research Inc., 1996.

Also consult the Job Bank series (Holbrook, Mass.: Adams Media Group). Adams Media publishes 18 separate guides about job opportunities in the following areas: Atlanta, Boston, Chicago, Dallas/Ft. Worth, Denver, Detroit, Florida, Houston, Los Angeles, Minneapolis, New York, Ohio, Philadelphia, Phoenix, San Francisco, Seattle, St. Louis, and Washington, D.C.

FINDING PLACES TO PRACTICE JOB SKILLS

An apprenticeship is an official opportunity to learn a specific profession by working side by side with a skilled professional. As a training method, it's as old as the hills, and it's making a comeback in a big way because people are realizing that doing a job is simply the best way to learn a job.

An internship is an official opportunity to gain work experience (paid or unpaid) in an industry of interest. Interns are more likely to be given entry-level tasks but often have the chance to rub elbows with people in key positions within a company. In comparison to an apprenticeship, which offers very detailed training for a specific job, an internship offers a broader look at a particular kind of work environment.

Both are great ways to learn the ropes and stay one step ahead of the competition. Consider it dress rehearsal for the real thing!

Cantrell, Will. *International Internships and Volunteer Programs.* Oakton, Va.: World Wise Books, 1992.

Guide to Apprenticeship Programs for Non-College Bound Youth. New York: Rosen, 1996.

Hepburn, Diane, ed. *Internships 1997.* Princeton, N.J.: Peterson's, 1997.

Summerfield, Carol J., and Holli Cosgrove. *Ferguson's Guide to Apprenticeship Programs: Traditional and Nontraditional.* Chicago: Ferguson's, 1994.

NO-COLLEGE OCCUPATIONS

Some of you will be relieved to learn that a college degree is not the only route to a satisfying, well-paying career. Whew! If you'd rather skip some of the schooling and get down to work, here are some books you need to consult.

Abrams, Kathleen S. *Guide to Careers Without College.* Danbury, Conn.: Franklin Watts, 1995.

Corwen, Leonard, *College Not Required!: 100 Great Careers That Don't Require a College Degree.* New York: Macmillan, 1995.

Curless, Maura. *Careers Without College: Kids.* Princeton, N.J.: Peterson's, 1993.

Farr, J. Michael. *America's Top Jobs for People Without College Degrees.* Indianapolis: JIST, 1997.

Longshore, Shirley. *Careers Without College: Office.* Princeton, N.J.: Peterson's, 1994.

Peterson, Linda. *Careers Without College: Entertainment.* Princeton, N.J.: Peterson's, 1994.

Unger, Harlow G. *But What If I Don't Want to Go to College?: A Guide to Success through Alternative Education.* Rev. ed. New York: Facts On File, 1998.

INDEX

Page numbers in **boldface** indicate main articles. Page numbers in *italics* indicate photographs.